More Innovative Redesign and Reorganization of Library Technical Services

Edited by Bradford Lee Eden

LIBRARIES
U N L I M I T E D
A Member of the Greenwood Publishing Group

Westport, Connecticut • London

Library of Congress Cataloging-in-Publication Data

More innovative redesign and reorganization of library technical
    services / edited by Bradford Lee Eden.
        p. cm.
    Includes bibliographical references and index.
    ISBN 978-1-59158-778-1 (alk. paper)
        1. Technical services (Libraries)—Management. 2. Technical services
    (Libraries)—Case studies. I. Eden, Bradford Lee.
    Z688.5.M67 2009
    025'.02—dc22   2008031209

British Library Cataloguing in Publication Data is available.

Library of Congress Catalog Card Number: 2008031209
ISBN: 978-1-59158-778-1

First published in 2009

Libraries Unlimited, 88 Post Road West, Westport, CT 06881
A member of the Greenwood Publishing Group, Inc.
www.lu.com

Printed in the United States of America

The paper used in this book complies with the
Permanent Paper Standard issued by the National
Information Standards Organization (Z39.48–1984).

10 9 8 7 6 5 4 3 2 1

Contents

Introduction

This book continues to explore the topic of innovative redesign and reorganization of library technical services departments. It can be considered a continuing volume of *Innovative Redesign and Reorganization of Library Technical Services: Paths for the Future and Case Studies* (Libraries Unlimited, 2004), as it examines more recent examples of technical services redesigns and reorganizations and also provides much more variety in the types of libraries and cultures represented.

The first chapter details how the Yarra Plenty Regional Library in Melbourne, Australia, adopted the "Brisbane" model and was able to completely disband its technical services department. In chapter 2, Elizabeth Brice and Ross Shanley-Roberts describe how the evolution of the job duties of the technical services librarian at Miami University in Oxford, Ohio, occurred, and they provide some tips for reorganization for other libraries. The movement from technical services to a collections management approach in a medical library is examined in chapter 3 by Dean James, Laurel Sanders, and Michael Garrett, as well as how the redesign of the library's Web site assisted in this reorganization. Survey results on technical services reorganization in law libraries are detailed by Karen A. Nuckolls in chapter 4. Hybrid positions and shared responsibilities of technical services and public services functions are described in chapter 5 by Laurie Phillips as a way to deal with decreased budgets, fewer staff, and more library responsibilities. A major reorganization and redesign of technical services at Northwestern University, which was accomplished innovatively and very quickly, is detailed in chapter 6 by Roxanne Sellberg. In chapter 7 Daniel Sifton shows that even a small, regional public library can effect change in technical services functions through simple workflow redesign. Vicki Toy Smith, a contributor to the original book, includes a follow-up in chapter 8 with another survey that examines the changing roles of librarians in technical services departments, and shows how much of this change is due to electronic resources. The final two chapters explore how Web 2.0 tools and services have been incorporated in technical services departments to promote efficiency, collaboration, and integration of services. An urban, bilingual community college library incorporates tagging, LibraryThing, Google Docs, and wikis into its library Web site, as documented by Elisabeth Tappeiner and Kate Lyons in chapter 9. Adam Murray's provocative and thought-inducing chapter 10 shows how free Web 2.0 tools have transformed the acquisitions and collections development process at

Murray State University in Kentucky, through the use of Google Docs, Google Spreadsheets, and LibraryThing.

It is hoped that this continuation of new ideas and workflows will provide practical support for library technical services department heads and staff to remain viable, functional, and important working units in today's libraries and larger institutions.

Bradford Lee Eden, Ph.D.
Associate University Librarian for Technical Services
and Scholarly Communication
University of California, Santa Barbara

1

Technical Services—Gone (and Forgotten)

Christine Mackenzie
Michael Aulich

Introduction

Technical services departments are part of the twentieth-century library, not the twenty-first. The days of every library having its own catalogers and processors are surely numbered, as library managers look for smarter ways of allocating resources, both human and fiscal.

By working in partnership with library suppliers, a seamless process has been devised in Australia whereby suppliers select items and catalog them directly into the library's database, then deliver them to the branches shelf ready. Detailed profiles are provided to ensure that the items selected meet the needs of each branch.

Overview

Robertson and Catoggio (2006) emphasize the difference between outsourcing and strategic procurement: "Strategic procurement is about finding the most effective, yet cost-efficient way of procuring goods or services. It's about using a structured framework to analyse what is happening now, define current and future needs, research the options, go to the market, negotiate an effective outcome and finally, ongoing management of the procurement process" (2006).

This chapter describes why Yarra Plenty Regional Library (YPRL) in Melbourne, Australia, adopted the "Brisbane model" and moved to strategic procurement of library materials in 2005. (The authors were responsible for developing the "Brisbane model" in 1999.) YPRL provides library services to

1

three local government authorities and is incorporated under the Victorian Local Government Act. It has eight branches and two mobile libraries and serves a population of 306,000.

Definitions

- Shelf-ready materials: library items cataloged, processed, and delivered directly to branches, ready to be placed on the shelf

- Supplier-aided selection: selection of titles by suppliers, using profiles or standing orders based on carefully prepared specifications

- "Brisbane model": term coined in Australia to describe the process of the supplier providing a seamless service from ordering through cataloging, adding to the library database, processing, and delivering items, coupled with supplier-aided selection, whereby the bulk of purchasing is conducted via profile or standing orders; based on the process used successfully by Brisbane City Council Library Services since 1999

Environmental Scan

In *Due for Renewal*, a national report on UK library services by the UK Audit Commission (1997), the acquisition of new stock was singled out as showing a wide variation in the total resources that authorities employ in this activity. Such differences primarily reflect variations in the purchase price, the cost of servicing the new stock, and the staff effort used to acquire it. According to the report, library authorities can take steps to reduce all of these costs.

More recently, a report by PriceWaterhouseCoopers for the Museums, Archives and Libraries Council in the UK (2006) outlined the key issues in improving stock procurement. Most of the recommendations in relation to selection of stock, procurement, processing and servicing, cataloging and delivery, and receipting are part of the Brisbane model, indicating world best practice. These recommendations are a solid endorsement of this methodology and process.

The *Strategic Asset Audit of Victorian Public Libraries*, an independent report conducted for the Library Board of Victoria and Victorian public library network by JL Management in 2006 (Liddle 2007) states that in-house cataloging was the favored approach by Victorian public libraries and accounted for 81.9 percent of new items. When viewed from an industry perspective, this represents considerable resource duplication. More than half (54.6 percent) of Victoria's forty-four library services reported that their work-in-process time (i.e., from receipt to shelf) is greater than twenty working days. Only three services achieve a turnaround time of one to five days.

Drivers

The opportunities that strategic procurement offers are the ability to move staff from the back end to the front end of the library, cost savings, improved delivery times, reduction in manual handling, and enhanced quality of products. It enables libraries to tap into the considerable experience and expertise of library suppliers, who have a wide and deep understanding of the publishing industry.

Strategic Direction

YPRL moved to strategic procurement in July 2005 as a result of a series of processes undertaken in 2004 to redefine the library service's direction. Through the planning process, functions were identified that had to be performed to achieve its goals. Many of these functions were new and based on programs and services that engage the community, build community capacity, and encourage reading and literacy. There was also an emphasis on the online environment and how online resources could be made more visible and accessible and be better promoted. Resources were reallocated from technical services to these functions, and the library service has been realigned and repurposed. The new Outreach Department comprises a manager, a local history librarian, a reading coordinator, a marketing and media coordinator, and an aged services librarian. These are all new positions in the library service.

Reducing Costs

The *Strategic Asset Audit* (Liddle 2007) comments:

> A common concern expressed when discussing libraries with non-librarian stakeholders is that resources appear to be wasted through duplicated effort in ordering and processing library materials . . . [this] was confirmed with the finding that 81.9 percent of new items are catalogued in-house . . . The average cost to procure a new item, from selection to shelf, was found to be $11.28 . . . Given that the average unit cost per item acquired was $20.19, the technical services component of $11.28 adds a further 56 percent to the cost of making an item available on library shelves. This is a considerable impost for tasks which, perhaps with the exception of selection and cataloguing, do not add value and clearly demonstrates that evaluation of alternate approaches could be beneficial.

The same report confirms the value of YPRL's decision to move to this process. The statewide average cost to procure a new item from selection to shelf was found to be $AUD11.28. YPRL's costs are below the state average, at $AUD7.06. The differential between the statewide average and YPRL's average, multiplied by the number of items acquired, shows a savings of $290,600 per annum, very close to the projected savings of $300,000 from a cost benefit analysis done to support the introduction of outsourcing.

Timeliness of Delivery

As well as saving money by moving to shelf ready, there are efficiencies in the speed of delivery of materials to branches. The supplier provides a seamless service, from ordering through cataloging, adding to the library database, then processing and delivering materials. Coupled with the shift to supplier-aided selection, in which the bulk of purchasing is done via profile or standing orders prepublication, considerable time savings is achieved. Customer needs are more effectively anticipated through surveys, and main drivers for demand are identified by scanning newspaper reviews, bookshop booklists, and television shows. This ensures the best chance of getting potential "hits" into the library ready for demand. Feedback from branches is that books reviewed in the weekend papers are already in the system. As previously mentioned, the average library takes more than twenty days to catalog and process materials; YPRL takes five days.

Technical Aspects

A successful approach to outsourcing requires a sound understanding of business principles, together with a commitment to engage with and value the skills of suppliers and work in partnership with them. The library and the supplier must agree that cataloging and processing is neither a loss leader nor a profit unit, but one of the requirements of doing business.

Well understood contract specifications mediated by individual customer service agreements will ensure that both customer and supplier understand clearly defined requirements. There is mutual interdependence for success: the library relies on the supplier running a successful business, and the supplier relies on the library committing previously agreed amounts for a particular time. The Brisbane model is based on the principle that libraries partner with their library suppliers, utilizing their business and market intelligence and acknowledging their expertise and skills.

Web ordering and sophisticated business-to-business (B2B) transactions enabled over the TCP/IP backbone, together with proper access and security mechanisms, mean that libraries can conduct all their technical services using e-commerce principles. The library material suppliers are responsible for entering the order in the database, sourcing the bibliographic record, maintaining authority control, and updating both the library's database to indicate status and the Australian National Bibliographic Database (ANBD) to record holdings. The item is sent directly from the supplier to the branch, where it is receipted against a packing slip and made available for loan by simply checking the item in.

Implicit in this model is that there are quality systems in place to ensure that the integrity of the database and the key performance indicators are being met.

This can be achieved through regular audits and checks by designated library staff.

It is critical that the strategic procurement process be well managed. This involves

- carefully prepared and monitored profiles for the selection of materials that are updated at least annually,

- regular auditing of items on order,

- measuring the timeliness of delivery of items, and

- measuring satisfaction with the collection by borrowers.

Critical Success Factors in Outsourcing

Critical success factors identified for strategic procurement relate in part to a library's collection development activities. Successful outsourcing of technical services has occurred when the following criteria are met.

- Selection can be managed by profiles and/or standing orders: Within the public library context, and acknowledging that the publishing trade is a business that markets a product, the combined business intelligence of book suppliers, publishers, and library patrons can be assimilated into

  - profile orders based on individual branch demographics and the interests of the community and
  - standing orders for popular authors/series.

  Evidence from BCCLS and YPRL proves that this is an effective and efficient way of obtaining library materials for a public library. Emerging trends and themes can be quickly taken up if the contracts and profiles are carefully written. This is a mature business practice, and it recognizes the skills and professionalism of library suppliers, publishers, librarians, and patrons.

- Acquisitions can be simplified and expedited through Web ordering techniques and procedures: EDI (Electronic Data Interchange) protocols have never matured sufficiently to gain any true market acceptance within library systems. They have now been superseded by e-commerce techniques. This has reached its nadir in secure Web ordering (e.g., on Amazon.com). It is now debatable whether library management system acquisition modules are justifiable. Library suppliers mount and maintain bibliographic databases replicating *Global Books in Print* from which secure orders and transactions can be conducted. The sophistication of these e-commerce processes means that all proper audit requirements can be met.

- High-quality bibliographic resources are available for downline loading from bureau sources (all library suppliers have access to these services): Bureau level bibliographic services such as OCLC and ANBD and supplier level bureau services such as Brodart have progressed from the traditional provision of card record copy cataloging to immediate downline loading from full MARC databases. These databases contain records representing the majority of published and to be published materials (most public libraries have a 98 percent hit rate). This common library practice has now migrated into enhanced services (e.g., abstracts, covers, blurbs, images, and sound bites)—fully fledged data streaming from remote servers and remote sources.

  This efficient and cost-effective method of obtaining high-grade catalog records can be easily coupled with the updating of national bibliographic databases meeting professional obligations and facilitating resource sharing. In Australia there is also a business return on this, and it can be cost neutral.

- Processing is well understood and kept to a minimum: The outcome of processing should be that library materials are protected and can be identified. Any requirements beyond this should be subject to close scrutiny.

- Shelf-ready provision is managed and costed as a business activity: To achieve the best possible major key performance indicators (i.e., cost, timeliness, and quality), the outsourcing relationship should be managed according to proper business practices and procedures. The relationship also needs to be a partnership, not simply a contractual one. There should be no duplication, so what staff are doing at the supplier end is not duplicated in the library, and library staff are not duplicating or embellishing supplier work. Positions must be clearly defined and quality assurance processes articulated and agreed to.

- Partnering principles and practices are well understood: Many businesses have assimilated their suppliers as full partners in their core business. Once this interdependence has been recognized, partnering practices based on understanding of business needs are used to maintain and further business ends.

- Contract specifications can be translated into customer service agreements (CSAs) between participating partners: The tender must be such that any contract deriving from it clearly specifies all mandatory requirements and standards. These can then be formulated into working CSAs, which include boundaries, standards, etc.

- Open communication and agreed change management are practiced: Contracts or CSAs cannot guarantee successful outcomes unless open communication channels and ongoing change management principles are applied. If they are not, the business relationship may fail. The importance of these intangibles cannot be overstated.

- TCP/IP backbone is available: This mode of B2B in e-commerce is predicated on fast, robust, and redundant Internet capabilities with 24/7 availability.

- Agreed quality control procedures are in place: Quality control is paramount. Minimum levels of AACR level 2, US MARC, and LCSH subject approach should be specified. The customer should independently monitor the quality of these inputs.

- Business-to-business and e-commerce principles can be applied in a secure manner (access control, authentication and verification, and secure transactions): Secure read/write access, which does not compromise other services, applications, or systems, must be implemented.

The market is such that the greatest efficiencies and cost effectiveness in outsourcing technical services are presently available within the public lending library business context. National and state libraries have statutory collecting requirements, which currently negate many efficiencies and economies of scale available from full shelf-ready products in public libraries. Academic and special libraries likewise have idiosyncratic collecting requirements, which preclude the real efficiencies of total shelf ready.

Key Factors in Selecting Suppliers

Suppliers must have the technical, management, physical, and financial resources to supply library materials as shelf-ready products. They have to demonstrate that they can

- place on-order records on the library management system;

- update holding records in both ANBD and the library management system;

- provide timely delivery of material from supplier to branch libraries;

- process books, nonbooks, and/or serials;

- supply a secure Web site for ad hoc ordering by authorized staff; and

- demonstrate their ability to manage and refine standing and profile orders to maximize usage of all library materials supplied to branch libraries.

As well as their expertise in the supply of shelf-ready library materials, suppliers need experience in the maintenance of ICT systems, including Web sites for material ordering, cataloging interfaces, and system security. Service quality issues that should be assessed include

- range of stock available;
- speed of supply;
- quality and extent of other (value-added) services offered;
- quality systems and/or certification;
- the ability to conform to customer requirements in regard to invoicing, etc.;
- references and reputation; and
- financial viability.

Quality Assurance

The model implies that staff members within the library service are responsible for ensuring the quality of the product delivered to the library. Quality includes all key performance indicators: time from supplier to library shelf, cost of cataloging and processing per item, processing quality, and cataloging standards. The library must be aware of and identify all processes undertaken. This requires investigating end-to-end processes, starting with the specifications for covering and finishing with financial accountabilities. Before outsourcing technical services, it is useful to reassess and pare down processes by looking at each step and asking, "Why are we doing this?"

Communication

Moving to this model requires careful planning and change management. Issues that can arise include the need to change processes, redeploy staff, manage quality control, retain sufficient skills in-house, and ensure that the library service is not exposed to risk in regard to suppliers' commercial viability. Much of the concern about moving to shelf-ready materials and supplier-aided selection is librarians' feeling that they will lose control of the process. This can be assuaged by including staff in the development of their branch profiles, encouraging customers to request titles for the library, and using statistical measures to strategically manage collections.

Funders appreciate the cost effectiveness and efficiencies gained by strategic procurement of library materials.

Conclusion

Customer service is paramount for public libraries. Restructuring and reengineering at both BCCLS and YPRL has been predicated on the assumption that it will provide better customer service and more effective use of resources, both financial and human. Moving to strategic procurement for library materials has enabled strategic outcomes to be achieved, delivered cost savings, and provided faster delivery of materials.

References

Liddle, John. 2007. *Strategic asset audit of Victorian public libraries: An independent report for the Library Board of Victoria and Victorian Public Library Network.* Available at http://www.slv.vic.gov.au/pdfs/aboutus/publications/strategic_audit_report.pdf (accessed September 4, 2008).

Museums, Libraries and Archives Council. 2006. *Better stock, better libraries: Transforming library stock procurement.* Phase 2 Final Report, August. Available at www.mla.gov.uk/resources/assets//B/better_stock_better_libraries_10123.pdf (accessed September 4, 2008).

Robertson & Catoggio. 2006. *Strategic procurement of library materials.* ALIA Conference Perth 2006. Available at conferences.alia.org.au/alia2006/Papers/Sharon_Robertson_Anita_Catoggio.pdf (accessed September 4, 2008).

UK Audit Commission. 1997. *Due for renewal: A report on the library service.* n.p.: Audit Commission for Local Authorities and the National Health Service in England and Wales.

2

Beyond the Catalog: The Evolution of the Technical Services Librarian at Miami University, Oxford, Ohio

Elizabeth Brice
Ross Shanley-Roberts

The technological transformation experienced by libraries in the past decade has had no greater impact than in technical services departments, where not only the tools being used but the materials being managed have changed dramatically. Having personnel equipped to respond to those changes and seize the opportunities that result is crucial, and there has been a growing discussion in the profession addressing these issues:

> Today's library technical services face the most significant changes since the invention of moveable type. These changes challenge librarians to develop new policies, apply new technologies, develop new competencies, and to take risks for making improvements. Most importantly, libraries find themselves operating in a totally new environment, one where they serve as only one source of information, not *the* source of information. Finding solutions involving policy changes cannot be outsourced. (Fessler 2007, 139)

It is time for technical services managers to rethink their expectations when hiring new professionals and identifying training opportunities for current librarians. Technical services staff, too often seen as the bastion of outmoded thinking and stubborn resistance to change, should be the source of new ideas, applications, tools, and innovative problem solving. To achieve this may require a change in how technical services librarians understand their mission, how they approach their execution of it, and how they advertise and fill positions. As

Calhoun noted, "People are the key to success. . . . A graduated, increasingly skilled use of information technology, together with resourcefulness and creativity, can be the engine of momentous advances in library technical services" (2003, 288).

This chapter is based largely on experiences at Miami University (Oxford, Ohio), where innovation and creative problem solving are highly valued and librarians with information technology skills are reshaping the services being offered to clients.

Same Mission, Different World

The fundamental mission of technical services—to provide the tools and expertise to organize and provide access to knowledge and information objects—has not changed, and given the persistence of print materials, for the immediate future librarians must still manage many of the same tasks performed for the last fifty years or more. In addition, technical services departments have been able to absorb with little difficulty the more recent tasks associated with providing access to electronic journals, cataloging online resources, maintaining a portal, etc. Calhoun likened these broadening responsibilities to a "three-ring circus," requiring technical services librarians to have more than just basic Web technology skills (2003, 284). But increasingly there is more for technical services staff to do. With the impact of social networking applications and the demand for both user-generated and user-centered content, the path to achieving that fundamental mission seems even more challenging.

At the same time, technical services librarians have been forced to reexamine their traditional tools and practices as the catalog itself has come under fire from both within and outside the technical services field. A flurry of reports on cataloging, from the University of California (Bibliographic Services Task Force 2005), Indiana University (Byrd 2006), and the Library of Congress (Calhoun 2006), sparked intense debates over the value of the bibliographic system that has been developed over the last century and a half, while a separate but related attack on the MARC record (Tennant 2002, 26, 28) led to widespread questions about its ultimate survival.

Whereas librarians need to stop confusing the catalog as bibliographic structure with the ILS system that provides access to it, technical services librarians must expand their view beyond the catalog. The catalog is in fact a tool for organization and access, and whether or not it continues to play the central role it has in the past, the need for organizing and providing access to information objects will not go away. The tools being used today may be revolutionized by technology tomorrow; perhaps in five years the "catalog" will no longer exist or will be unrecognizable compared with its current incarnation. But whatever the access tools needed for the future, it is not in the best interest of either the profession or the public to allow nonprofessionals or commercial enterprises to determine the future of information access. Technical services librarians must be part of both the debate and the solutions.

To have a hope of achieving the technical services mission and of making valuable contributions in the new environment, the field of technical services needs librarians who combine some of the traditional expertise of information organization and access with competencies in information technology/Web 2.0 skills, project management, user studies, and collaboration. Librarians for whom innovation is a state of mind, a part of their daily thought processes and central to problem solving, will be key players in the twenty-first-century library. Identifying and developing these individuals may require creative thinking and efforts from managers, but this investment of time and effort is crucial to the long-term health of the profession.

Miami University Libraries

The experience at the Miami University Libraries during the past twenty years can serve as a useful model for many other libraries, especially similar medium-sized academic libraries. Like others, Miami has seen a dramatic difference in how technical services have been provided over the last twenty years.

In 1985 separate Acquisitions and Cataloging Departments existed to purchase and catalog a collection that was overwhelmingly print based. The Acquisitions Department was entirely concerned with ownership, and preorder searching was a lengthy process that resulted in a large backlog. Another large backlog of books awaited cataloging. Long-standing procedures were seldom questioned, and the two departments rarely discussed workflow. Only catalog librarians and one or two highly experienced senior staff did copy cataloging; support staff were truly clerical. Their work was limited to inputting the many editing changes librarians made to records, using dumb terminals that uploaded records to OCLC. Staff and student assistants maintained a large card catalog. The work of librarians was stable and limited by today's standards; they focused on copy and original cataloging—there was much more of that then—and advised the head cataloger on policy decisions. Quality cataloging was defined as the production of very detailed records that required a thorough if not perfectionist approach. The organizational culture of the department was hierarchical and rigid.

By 1990 this era of the "traditional" technical services librarian had changed dramatically. A new dean was hired to automate the Libraries, and after much work, Miami migrated to an online catalog and an integrated library system. The OhioLINK consortia's innovative cooperative catalog, which enabled the sharing of collections among Ohio academic libraries, became a reality. Smart workstations enabled catalog librarians to input their own changes, freeing the support staff to take on simple copy cataloging. E-journals were emerging, along with early experiments with e-books and digital technologies.

The organizational response to this new electronic environment was to combine the individual processing departments into the Technical Services Department. Both the dean and the assistant university librarian strongly supported innovation, and by 1995 the head of technical services began a complete reengineering of the department workflow. He had recognized that the tasks traditionally performed in the department were beginning to subvert the department's mission. The goals of reengineering were to reestablish the primacy of the department's mission and identify new ways to achieve it through the elimination of unnecessary and duplicate procedures, the improvement of efficiency, the more effective use of staff resources, and the freeing of librarians to assume more challenging roles. Underlying this approach was a willingness to rethink every policy, process, procedure, and assumption, which would prove key to enabling innovation in the development of new workflows.

The principles of total quality management (TQM) then being implemented throughout the library system empowered both librarians and support staff to be involved in the envisioning of the future of their work and the department. As reengineering progressed the traditional functional division between acquisitions and cataloging became blurred. Now the new order team was bringing in cataloging records from OCLC and the new receipt team, composed of copy catalogers rather than the acquisitions staff, was receiving the books. This long and difficult process was ultimately a success. The new team-based organizational structure resulted in the almost complete elimination of order and cataloging backlogs, which led to a sense of pride as support staff took ownership for much of the workflow and librarians were freed to do more complex and challenging work. The new culture encouraged a freer flow of ideas from all levels, and librarians especially were encouraged to seek continuous improvement.

During this same time Miami hired the current special projects technologist as authority control librarian. Encouraged by the support for innovation at the Libraries, he began experimenting with automating the authority control processing and as a result drastically reduced the time required to fulfill those duties. He was then freed to begin investigating digitizing, scripting, and database creation and was able to combine these new skills when the digital processing unit was created and placed under his supervision. This unit was responsible for the scanning and maintaining of Miami's electronic reserves and for the digitizing of library materials. When the technologist took a leave of absence the unit passed to the leadership of another innovative librarian, who transferred into technical services from public services to take on the challenge of evolving this unit into the current Digital Initiatives Department. Now the metadata librarian works closely with Digital Initiatives to provide access to growing digital collections.

With these examples, and with the encouragement of both the former and the current department head, technical services librarians at Miami have continued to seek innovative means to solve problems and create new tools. They have used a combination of traditional and information technology skills to increase support staff's productivity in the traditional areas of ordering and cataloging by using macros and Web scripting, freeing staff for activities that require more knowledge and judgment-based decision making. They have created online databases to help selectors manage major serials review and cancellation projects and collection inventories. They are looking for ways to exploit Web 2.0 applications and investigating different avenues to increase access to the catalog and to incorporate the catalog into new social networking tools. This work has exposed much of the richness of the MARC record that the commercial ILS never did. With increased access to previously unusable data comes an increased need to identify and correct errors, revisit earlier policy decisions, and enhance records. They are also looking to make as much use of FRBR and the disaggregation of the elements of works (chapters, articles, illustrations, etc.) as possible to increase the level of specificity and interrelatedness of searches. These efforts will require the combined skills of catalogers, database maintenance staff, and technologically savvy technical services librarians who may not necessarily do any of the traditional tasks of technical services. With every opportunity Miami is looking to hire people who have the background, training, and interest to make innovation a significant part of their jobs.

Focus on the Mission, Not the Job

It is all too easy for technical services librarians to associate their responsibilities with the daily job, rather than with the mission of their organization, but identifying too closely with one's job can be self-defeating. In this chaotic environment the longer one works at any one institution, the more likely one's job is going to change. The reality is that there is an unending opportunity for technical services librarians to apply professional expertise to new situations, but recognizing those opportunities may require a mental shifting of gears and a willingness to let go of familiar, comfortable activities. Increasing interconnectivity and interoperability means that commercially available materials will not need to be handled by local technical services librarians much longer. There is already a clear sense that much of traditional technical services work can and should be performed using shared information, such as vendor-supplied cataloging, aggregated periodicals, and Google-ized electronic versions of older print materials. This should be a clarion call to any beginning or mid-career technical services librarians that although traditional activities will not end as long as there are analog materials, the decrease in time required means that librarians should be honing other skill sets.

But the nature of technical services librarians has always been much more that of generalist than specialist. They should focus on where the needs are and move to meet them. They need to come out from behind the walls of the technical services department, their offices, and their cubicles and interact with local client communities face to face. They should support clients by serving as conduits between the information clients seek, the content they create, and the broader world with which they want to communicate. To do that, technical services librarians must listen; study client needs, expectations, and behaviors; and design applications that are appropriate to them.

Ordering books, checking in journals, and cataloging monographs are no longer the work of librarians in most institutions. Instead, technical services librarians must work with commercial content producers to develop business models and practices that are reasonable and effective for everyone. They have to develop effective and efficient rights management tools. They must analyze, design, and modify a variety of interface applications to provide improved context-based search and discovery for their clients, basing their designs on extensive user studies. They have to partner with a variety of colleagues, both inside and outside the library, to offer instruction, assistance, coordination, and design for metadata applications in such areas as library digital collections, institutional repositories, and targeted user communities. And they must understand and exploit the strengths of social networking applications to make the library visible, accessible, and useful.

As budgets continue to tighten, especially in higher education, units that cannot demonstrate their value will be sacrificed in favor of those that can. Technical services professionals can no longer assume that library administrators will support them if they continue to do business as usual. Instead they must demonstrate the value of having librarians with the skills to create new tools to improve access to collections, who can work capably with digital resources and respond to the rapid changes in this new environment, who understand metadata and how to structure it, and who drive library innovations in knowledge access.

Foster a Culture Supportive of Innovation

If technical services librarians genuinely seek to play a role in the evolving information environment, they have to work now to establish departmental, and indeed library, cultures that support the development of this new breed of technical services professional. This culture must be open to ideas from everyone, reward innovation, value creative problem solving, encourage experimentation and risk taking, tolerate failure, generate broad awareness of environmental changes, redefine "quality" to include expectations for on-demand delivery and client convenience, value cost effectiveness, and create excitement about the future and the library's role in it.

Although the technical services department traditionally has been a production environment, managers must consider the value and advantages of providing time and support for "R&D." Providing the resources to investigate new tools and applications is an investment in the future of library services and should not be limited to any one area of the library. Ongoing exploration is in the strategic interest of the entire library community, and the technical services mission can provide a good foundation for much of the work that remains to be done.

Recruit and Hire for the Potential to Innovate

Although culture is important, it is ultimately individuals that drive change. In Miami's case it was a library administrator who has not only supported but advocated and pushed for new ideas, tools, techniques, and practices and hired the expertise to provide it; a department head who recognized that the past is not a useful predictor of the future and the excuse "because we've always done it that way" almost always indicates a need for review and updating; and a librarian whose first act upon being hired was to automate almost all of his job, enabling him to pursue more innovative and challenging pursuits.

Managers must play a key role in the evolution of their staff and should begin by looking beyond the traditional skill sets sought by technical services departments when hiring. They should rethink the competencies they need and advertise for; to date technical services managers have been slow in reformulating positions to match the new reality (Fessler 2007, 143). Traditional skills may still be needed but should be enhanced by Web 2.0 skills and other competencies. And managers should encourage professional educators to advance their curricula for technical services. Professional programs must help students understand not only the principles of information organization and access, but also the information technology tools being used to actualize those principles and the realities of the new workplace, where project management, partnering, and collaboration are key (Fessler 2007, 143). Libraries are starting to see more graduates with these competencies, but few graduates are seeing the potential for their skills in technical services. Technical services departments will need a regular infusion of new graduates who understand the latest technological developments to help educate current staff. They will need librarians who understand Web 2.0 applications, the needs and expectations of the Web 2.0 users who are today's students and increasingly today's faculty, and the changing landscape of the scholarly communications environment.

To develop this type of workforce may require some innovative approaches. At Miami, Dean Judith Sessions has successfully used short-term residency positions to offer new librarians opportunities for exploration, growth, and collaboration across departmental lines. This approach has resulted in permanent positions for a number of residents. Experimenting with new types of employment, such as telecommuting and cross-departmental assignments, may also be valuable in creating a more flexible staff that is open to new ideas.

The management of librarians with the sought-after competencies requires multiple and ongoing efforts (Shaughnessy 1992, 282–98). A new hire's master's degree is only the beginning of competency development and must be followed by a continuous application of mentoring, self-study, continuing education, collegial interaction, and experimentation. Technical services managers must create opportunities for librarians to continually upgrade their skills, continue their education, and share their learning with others, to the benefit of all.

Conclusion

It is now sufficiently clear that technical services librarians cannot be complaisant about their role in the library profession, the perceived value of their expertise, and the acknowledged importance of the service they provide to library clients. It is also clear that there is a tremendous opportunity for technical services professional to demonstrate their value and make genuine contributions to facilitate their clients' experience in the new information environment. Karen Calhoun has laid out an ambitious agenda for the "metadata specialist" of the twenty-first century: there is much work and much opportunity to wield professional expertise ahead (2007, 174–85).

To do so effectively, the field of technical services will need innovative people who are eager to explore the knowledge environment of the future, support client-created content, foster client-centered collections, wield a variety of content standards, fashion new responses to new problems, and serve their mission in an ambiguous and constantly changing landscape. The future for technical services is indeed an exciting one.

References

Beall, Jeffrey. 2006. Stop the war on metadata. *Library Journal* 131 (12): 46.

Bibliographic Services Task Force. 2005. *Rethinking how we provide bibliographic services for the University of California.* Final report, December. libraries.universityofcalifornia.edu/sopag/BSTF/Final.pdf (accessed September 4, 2008).

Byrd, Jackie, et al. 2006. *A white paper on the future of cataloging at Indiana University.* January 15. www.iub.edu/~listserv/pub/Future_of_Cataloging_White_Paper.pdf (accessed September 4, 2008).

Calhoun, Karen. 2003. Technology, productivity and change in library technical services. *Library Collections, Acquisitions, & Technical Services* 27 (3): 281.

Calhoun, Karen. 2006. *The changing nature of the catalog and its integration with other discovery tools: Prepared for the Library of Congress.* Final report, March 17. www.loc.gov/catdir/calhoun-report-final.pdf (accessed September 4, 2008).

Calhoun, Karen. 2007. Being a librarian: Metadata and metadata specialists in the twenty-first century. *Library Hi Tech* 25 (2): 174–87.

Fessler, Vera. 2007. The future of technical services (It's not the technical services it was). (cover story). *Library Administration & Management* 21 (3): 139–55.

Fisher, William. 2001. Core competencies for the acquisitions librarian. *Library Collections, Aquisitions, & Technical Services* 25 (2): 179–90.

Hall-Ellis, Sylvia D. 2006. Descriptive impressions of managerial and supervisory cataloger positions as reflected in American libraries, AutoCAT, and the Colorado State Library Jobline, 2000–2004: A content analysis of education, competencies, and experience. *Cataloging & Classification Quarterly* 42 (1): 55–92.

Marcum, Deanna B. 2006. The future of cataloging. *Library Resources & Technical Services* 50 (1): 5–9.

Medeiros, Norm. 2005. Factors influencing competency perceptions and expectations of technical services administrators. *Library Resources & Technical Services* 49 (3): 167–74.

Schadle, Steve, and Karen Calhoun. 2003. Preparing catalogers for the 21st century. *Technicalities* 23 (6): 6–7.

Shaughnessy, Thomas W. 1992. Approaches to developing competencies in research libraries. *Library Trends* 41 (Fall): 282–98.

Tennant, Roy. 2002. MARC must die. *Library Journal* 127 (17): 26, 28.

3

From Technical Services to Collections Management: The Evolution of Technical Services in a Medical Library

Dean James
Laurel Sanders
Michael Garrett

The Houston Academy of Medicine–Texas Medical Center (HAM–TMC) Library, founded in 1949, serves the educational, research, and clinical programs of the Texas Medical Center (TMC). The TMC is home to more than forty member institutions, including two medical schools,[1] three schools of nursing,[2] thirteen hospitals,[3] and more. The Library also serves as a resource for the greater Houston area and five states through its designation as the Regional Medical Library for National Network of Libraries of Medicine South Central Region (NN/LM SCR). Currently, the Collections Management Department bears responsibility for the selection, acquisition, cataloging, processing, and maintenance of resources. Selection of materials for the Library's historical collections is the responsibility of the associate director of the McGovern Historical Collections & Research Center, but collections management personnel acquire and catalog these materials. The present staff complement of the department consists of the associate director, three librarians, and four paraprofessionals, a total of eight full-time employees (FTE).

The organization of technical services functions in the HAM–TMC Library has changed several times over the past twenty-two years, beginning with the implementation of the Library's first online catalog and automated serials control system.[4] The current organization of the department reflects the evolution of technical services over the past twenty years, with ever-increasing emphasis on electronic resources. As long as the vast majority of the library's resources were print based rather than electronic, technical services personnel had simply to acquire, catalog, and process the items, then put them on the appropriate shelves, to make them available to users.[5] As the shift to electronic resources has developed, those same technical services staff have had to develop new skills and to rethink regularly how best to provide access to resources that do not reside conveniently on a shelf in the library. Whereas access to a library's collections once came through printed cards in a catalog, then via computerized versions of those cards in an OPAC, technological advances spurred by the advent of the Internet and the World Wide Web have revolutionized the way users access a library's collections. A library's "collection" includes far more than physical items residing within its walls.

Over the past two decades the technical services division at the HAM–TMC Library has followed the general trends as the functions of the departments have evolved. As technology has changed and affected the division's work, so has the scope of the division's mission and purpose changed. No longer is the purpose of technical services personnel simply to acquire, catalog, process, and house the items. Now the department actively seeks new and innovative means of delivering content to a vast and varied user group. Cataloging, acquisitions, and serials staff, aided by the expertise of a new database and Web services developer,[6] a librarian who joined the department in January 2006, are taking the department beyond its technical services roles, in the traditional sense, and striding into the world of Library 2.0.

This chapter discusses the history of the technical services division at the HAM–TMC Library from 1985 to the present. Because of the importance of the journal literature in a medical and scientific library environment, the chapter also examines in some detail the changes in the serials department during this time. The third part of the chapter provides an overview of the steps the department is taking to make innovative delivery of content a reality for the Library's users.

Part I: An Overview of Technical Services/Collections Management, 1986–2007

During fiscal year 1983–1984[7] the Library was preparing for the installation of its new automated system, the first phase of which was putting catalog records into electronic form. At the time the Technical Services Division consisted of three departments: Collection Development, Acquisitions (which included Serials), and Cataloging. Each department was headed by a librarian who reported to the assistant director for technical services.[8] By FY 1986–1987 the Library had implemented the LS/2000 ILS and had begun to use the SC350 module (a component of the LS/2000 ILS) for check-in of journals. Use of these automated systems brought about a major reorganization in technical services, the better to take advantage of the ILS's capabilities. Serials functions were reorganized, and the new Serials Department was created. The Acquisitions Department was subsumed into the Collection Development Department. It was also at this point that the Library became part of a local consortium, sharing its online catalog with three other libraries in the TMC.[9] The Cataloging Department no longer produced catalog cards, though the card catalog remained in place for a while longer.[10] The division's staff complement at this time consisted of 4.5 FTE librarians and 9 FTE paraprofessionals.

The Technical Services Division, still designated as such, retained its three-department organization for the next several years, until FY 1992–1993. At that point, the assistant executive director for collections and technical services served as the collection development officer and coordinated the activities of two departments, Cataloging and Serials, each with a librarian as department head.[11] In December 1992 the Serials Department stopped any form of manual check-in by doing away with its Kardex.[12] Prior to this, problems with the serials control module and the ILS had precluded such a move.

For a number of years the Library's collection development officer received input from a Serials Selection Committee in making decisions about acquiring new titles and canceling others. In FY 1993–1994 this committee changed its name to the Information Resources Committee (IRC) in recognition of the advent of a variety of electronic formats and methods of access besides print. The IRC created a subcommittee, the Internet Working Group, which would be responsible for identifying sources of information on the Internet. Connections to any selected databases were made easily available to the Library's users through menu choices in the online catalog. There were also several changes to workflow in the Technical Services Division. For one, the monograph acquisitions process became fully automated for the first time. Second, the negotiation of licenses to electronic products became a regular part of the serials acquisitions process.[13] Third, the overall structure of the division changed with the departure of the director of serials. At this point the director of cataloging took over management of the Serials Department, a process made much easier by the continued streamlining of divisional workflow.[14] The staff complement now consisted of 2 FTE librarians and 8 FTE paraprofessionals.[15]

During this same fiscal year (1993–1994) the Library implemented its first World Wide Web home page.[16] This Web site allowed users to connect to the Library's online catalog and to link to MEDLINE and a number of other databases, as well as to other libraries. The Internet Working Group was the primary selector for resources made available via the Web, and the creation and maintenance of the Web site were handled outside the Technical Services Division. From this point on Internet-accessible resources became increasingly important to the Library's users, and an ever greater percentage of the collections budget was consumed by serials, indexes, and databases (both electronic and print). As a consequence, the amount of money available for the purchase of print monographs steadily decreased. Fluctuations in the Library's budget during this period often necessitated the cancellation of significant numbers of serial titles, and the rapid and continual rise in serial prices made cuts seem even deeper (see figures 3.1 and 3.2). By FY 2002–2003 the Library had cancelled its long-standing approval plan for monograph acquisitions, and monograph purchases were limited to titles supporting educational programs and specific research projects.[17]

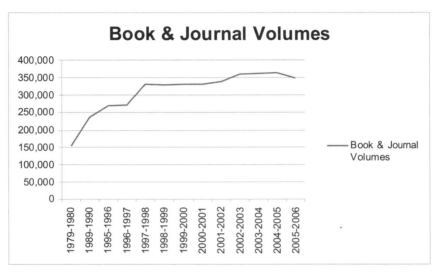

Figure 3.1. Acquisition of Print Resources Leveled off by 1998.

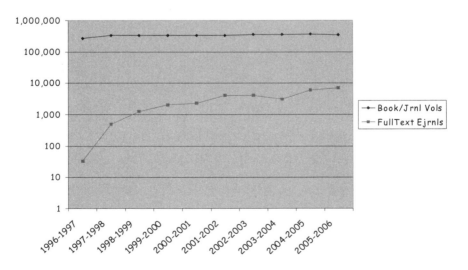

Figure 3.2. Comparative Growth Rates of Book and Bound Journal Volumes and Full-Text Electronic Journals.

Between September 26 and October 12, 2004, the Library undertook the first truly significant revision of its Web site since its inception nearly a decade before, implementing Serials Solutions® during this same period. In addition to making it easier for users to find materials and information resources, the new Web site featured a Serials Solutions® search box, which facilitated easy access to online journals.[18] Providing users with a highly functional entry point to the electronic-format journal literature became increasingly important in the intervening decade. Because of the signal importance of journal literature to the medical and scientific fields, a detailed examination of changes in the acquisition and provision of serials, both electronic and print, is necessary.

Part II: Serials at HAM–TMC Library, 1997–2007

Journals are the most essential resource for a medical and scientific community like the Texas Medical Center (TMC). Although serials work has changed radically at the HAM–TMC Library over the past decade, the same number of staff—three—has ensured access to journals during that time. During FY 1997–1998 there was no serials librarian position, although there had been until about 1993. Instead the department had a lead serials assistant who performed tasks normally allocated to a librarian. There were a check-in and claims specialist and a bindery specialist to handle approximately 4,100 print serial subscriptions. By the time the lead assistant left in 1998, she had begun pursuing and implementing online access for serials. By then, the Library Web site linked its users to about 230 journals, more than half of which consisted of tables of contents and abstracts; not many more than a hundred provided full text. The online versions often provided only part of the content found in print. Electronic access to journals was still free or provided at minimal cost (most often an additional 10 percent) with a print subscription. The Library's Webmaster (not a member of the department) administered e-journals as an HTML list, with the only contribution from the department being to alert the Webmaster to the availability of new titles. Few users complained when e-journal Web sites failed or links broke; in fact, many users seemed hardly aware of their existence.

In 1999 users still relied heavily on the print journal collection. The Library was often crowded and always busy, mostly with patrons locating and photocopying articles. Reference, serials, and interlibrary loan staff expended much effort in helping patrons locate print issues, and reshelving journals kept the shelving staff constantly busy. The OPAC was the most up-to-date access point for print journals, but some users still preferred to consult a printed holdings list produced semiannually from OCLC. Electronic holdings were not yet being entered in the catalog, further limiting awareness of their availability.

By February 1999, the Library's online journal collection had tripled to over 600 titles. At the beginning of 2000, there were 1,300 electronic journals in the collection; by the end of 2001, the Library suddenly had access to nearly

4,000. Maintaining the HTML list was fast becoming a full-time job; the Webmaster now jokingly referred to himself as "journal wrangler." The Library had begun participating in several University of Texas System consortial purchases of bundled electronic journals from major STM publishers and was also partaking of access to a large aggregated collection purchased by the Texas State Library. In December 2002 a new database-driven and dynamically updated electronic resources links page on the Web site provided access to 2,363 e-journals,[19] thanks to a custom-made SQL database developed by a new member of the IT staff. The Webmaster had departed in August, and not long afterward the staff member who created the database also left. The SQL database was now the responsibility of the serials librarian. No staff still at the Library had expertise in writing SQL, so the legacy database's structure could not be modified. Due to budget problems, complete cancellation of some titles duplicated by another TMC consortium library was negotiated with a publisher, resulting in complete loss of online access to those titles in 2003. Many of the Library's users reacted with displeasure at the prospect of walking into the Library or having to wait longer for articles, which surprised some librarians. As part of the effort to save funds, the head of Collections[20] negotiated with Wiley to convert subscriptions to online-only format, a move that seemed risky in terms of permanent access.

To manage its growing collection of online serials more efficiently, the Library purchased the Serials Solutions® A-Z list in July 2003. This was deemed advantageous, because it would present users with an interface for electronic journals that was both functional and attractive and provide serials staff with an easier-to-update, safely hosted, searchable serials list. By this time, however, the department was short a leader, and the serials database was tabled until it could be populated over the following summer. It was launched, along with a new version of the Web site, October 1, 2004.

A series of budget shortfalls after the turn of the millennium meant corresponding cancellations of journal titles over several fiscal years. In FY 2003–2004 Collections Management identified a list representing 25 percent of serials expenditures for cancellation. After the cancellation list was published on the Web site, resulting in much user feedback and revision of the list, cancellation of 370 print journals was effected in December, resulting in total loss of current access for 225 of them. Most publishers still required maintenance of a print subscription in return for online access, now in increasing demand, and most had also realized the financial wisdom in charging substantial fees for e-access. The Library maintained print even when optional for all titles retained, with the exception of the already cancelled Wiley print titles, primarily because the Library's extensive journal collection is a major regional and local resource, and there was a climate of uncertainty about the long-term availability of aging online issues. Publishers at the time generally made no guarantee to provide continuing access to older content in the event of a title's cancellation, and the "rolling access" model had been introduced, threatening to become standard fare. The first few years of the new millennium were a period of difficult transition for publishers, libraries, and end-users.

In 2005 budget problems resurfaced, due to a combination of flat funding and the rising cost of e-journals and databases. Publishers continued to experiment with changing their pricing models to better capture revenue from institutions, particularly those with large user populations like the HAM–TMC Library. E-journals had evolved, providing more user-friendly interfaces, more reliable infrastructure, accommodation of IP-based access in most cases, complete full text, and, increasingly, added-value features in online versions. Many publishers were responsive to libraries' fears about continued access, adding assurances, albeit vaguely worded ones, addressing this issue. More publishers began to digitize older content. These factors, along with programs like LOCKSS, the advent of open-access publishing, and publishers' adoption of policies making older content freely accessible to subscribers (and sometimes to the public), contributed to the Library's increased confidence in making the move to online-only access for the majority of its serials. The Library purchased an electronic resources management tool (ERMS) from Serials Solutions® and launched it after another summer of intensive data entry on the part of the serials librarian. The associate director for collections management had negotiated and joined consortium contracts for many more database licenses, herself creating and maintaining a database list on a separate Web page. The Library also began acquiring e-books. The serials librarian was still responsible for ensuring remote access of all resources by communicating changes and additions to the proxy administrator via a detailed spreadsheet, a procedure long used for updating online journals in the proxy server.

Until the Library dropped most print subscriptions for the 2007 subscription year, there was little opportunity to train staff to take over new e-resource management support roles. Their days were still largely taken up with accustomed tasks dealing with print publications. As of early 2006, the serials librarian and IT proxy administrator had been the only staff with any hands-on electronic journal experience for several years, during which they had collaborated to provide access to a collection of e-journals and databases that now numbers between 10,000 and 15,000 titles. Because of the inherent complexities among the Library's user community—institutions, firewalls, browser settings, multilevel remote access authentication, subscription and publisher glitches—access issues are time consuming and difficult to diagnose. Some technical background, as well as a careful, step-by-step interview with the affected user, is required to identify and begin to solve a problem. Because reference staff usually have needed to forward questions to serials staff, a department-based help desk service was instituted in 2006 to troubleshoot common user access problems. This has allowed the serials librarian more production time. After training, two support staff members are successfully aiding users, thereby also increasing their own understanding of virtual services and their vital importance to the TMC. E-mailed inquiries about access problems, many from public services staff or faculty, are still forwarded to the proxy administrator, the serials librarian, or the AD for collections to handle.

A flat budget for 2007 prompted the definitive move away from print. The serials librarian and the check-in assistant spent most of their time in the summer and fall of 2006 populating a huge spreadsheet to analyze all subscribed titles for usage, quality of e-access, availability of e-only access, cost-per-use of print versus electronic versions, impact factor, local authorship, and index coverage. Meanwhile, pricing models continued to change until the last minute, complicating the effort to predict whether the savings goal would ultimately be enough to offset price increases. In the end, all but about 280 print serials were cancelled for electronic-only access in 2007. About 250 more titles were cancelled completely. This time, virtually no objection has been heard from the Library's user community. In fact, many wondered why the Library had not already cancelled its print, as they now felt it was of no consequence to them. As the Library neared the end of FY 2006–2007, serials staff grappled with the implementation and integration of new technologies, a changing set of goals, and the question of how best to employ full-time support staff whose work with print resources would shortly all but disappear. The librarian position acquired a new title, "Serials and Electronic Resources Librarian," and a new librarian position, electronic resources coordinator, was filled at the beginning of FY 2007–2008. Under current planning, the serials and electronic resources librarian will continue to exchange information with the proxy manager; manage licenses and renewals for e-journals and e-journal packages; ensure accessibility of all serial resources; further implement and update the evolving ERMS; track electronic and print expenditures (with data input and invoice processing being handled by the check-in assistant); gather and analyze usage statistics; and, in accordance with a pending policy, enter more e-holdings in the catalog. The check-in assistant has been performing more varied electronic journal maintenance tasks, including some ERMS data entry and the help desk, and does data gathering for the various special projects that arise.[21] The check-in assistant took over the maintenance of PubMed LinkOut in 2006, a function that will change or end when the Library's link resolver is implemented in PubMed. The electronic resources coordinator will implement a federated search tool, continue to deploy the open-URL link resolver in more resources, help to negotiate licensing and maintain the databases and the database list, perform marketing and education functions (branding of resources, creation of tutorials), and investigate and help implement new methods of realizing the goal of a seamless and increasingly personalized user experience via the Library's Web site and through the educational institutions' courseware. The bindery assistant is nearing the end of her long experience as such, sending off the last large collection of issues to be bound; her time has recently been divided between serials projects, such as maintaining the Library's holdings in the SerHold/DocLine database, and new tasks, such as document scanning for a digital archiving project.

Between 1997 and 2007, HAM–TMC Library made considerable progress in presenting access to its electronic resources, but much of what the Library currently intends is not yet fully realized. During the period 1997–2003, the Library remained behind the curve in effecting the transition from print to electronic access. The term *innovation* could be applied only within the Library's own narrow context, and changes were made slowly and usually reactively. The Library's sense of its archival function, both regionally and locally, led it to cling to traditional resources until finances could no longer support this approach, and the department continued to apply support staff's efforts almost exclusively in the print arena. Several lapses in staffing key positions at various leadership levels throughout the Library occurred during this period, exacerbating the problem of conceiving and implementing a coherent and unified vision of the department's future path. Change during this period was forced chiefly by circumstance. In serials, one of the most labor-intensive and crucial areas, it seemed there was no time to stop and train support staff to integrate them into the process. From 2004 to 2007, however, much was accomplished, though not without some lingering internal resistance. Although the department is still catching up to the Library's users' current expectations, it is also actively engaged with forming a picture of the Library's future, a vision all recognize must continually be refocused in accordance with technological developments that can enhance the access and presentation of information resources. Current plans for electronic resources include a fuller implementation of the Library's open-URL link resolver, more ubiquitous branding, true federated searching, presentation of resources bundled for different user populations, and creation of subject-based interfaces that will also allow the individual user to choose some of the resources on view. The department will continue to work on bringing the Library to the user in every way possible, not least by integrating its collections and services into the online curriculum resources of the educational institutions that depend on the department. The HAM–TMC Library is evolving into an organization that is flexible and accepting of constant change, and that welcomes fresh opportunities to expand service to its users in innovative ways.

Part III: Extending the Vision

Simply providing access to resources is important, but just as important in a virtual world is how the content is delivered. A search of the online catalog or an index no longer suffices. Users today want to be able to search simultaneously as many sources of information as possible to achieve the results they want. In a move to be proactive in this regard, in January 2006 the Collections Management Department hired a librarian to serve as database and Web services developer. The redesign of the Library's Web site was the first step in a continual process of redesigning and implementing new ways for the Library to deliver content to its users.

Prior to October 1, 2006, the Library's external Web site was strictly static, scripted only with HTML. (See figures 3.3 and 3.4.) In such an environment, all the information in a file is retrieved each time the file is requested—the way a file server works. This environment obviously limits a user's ability to interact with the site's content because all content is predefined by the content providers. In addition, static Web pages are created manually; as a particular Web page needs to be updated, that file must first be accessed by the Web site's content manager, the necessary changes must be made, and finally the newly edited file must be uploaded to the server. Thus, as each new static Web page is added, the management aspect of that information increases. Because of the burgeoning wealth of important HAM–TMC Library information and the lack of interactivity/searching capabilities within the HAM–TMC Library's Web site, a more workable Web content solution needed to be implemented. That solution meant moving the existing Web site from its static environment to a dynamic, data-driven one in which data are fetched from a plethora of different sources.

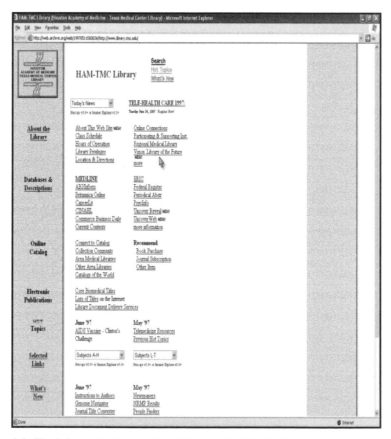

Figure 3.3. The Library's Former Web Site, HAM–TMC Library Screenshot, May 11, 1997. Courtesy of the Internet Archive (www.archive.org).

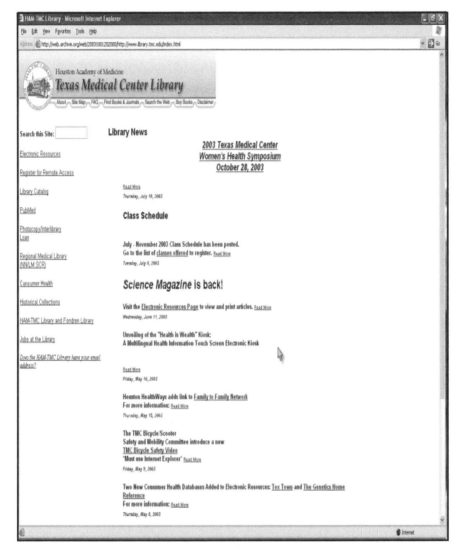

Figure 3.4. The Library's Former Web Site, HAM–TMC Library Screenshot, October 1, 2003. Courtesy of the Internet Archive (www.archive.org).

To achieve this move, it was necessary to add a Web application server to the Library's existing Web server architecture. A Web application server is a piece of software that extends the Web server, enabling it to perform activities it otherwise is incapable of—such as interacting with a database or sending e-mail—hence the name "application server." One can think of a Web application server's interaction with data as creating an environment in which a Web browser is not simply a piece of software used only to display HTML, but an interface *into* a particular application.

This additional piece of software does add complexity to a Web site. For instance, a Web application server requires its own special set of "language" or "scripting" constructs to be able to process different activities as it is queried. Its main activity is to serve as the middleware between the Web server and databases or other data sources.[22] The HAM–TMC Library decided to purchase Adobe's ColdFusion MX7 software as its application server technology. This decision was based on some important factors inherent in ColdFusion:

- ColdFusion's ability to run on multiple platforms. Previous use had shown the Library's IT staff the vulnerability of Microsoft's Internet Information Services (IIS) 6.0 Web server. Because of these experiences, the IT staff had decided to decommission the Windows Web server and replace it with a Linux server running the open-source, freely available Apache Web Server.[23]

- ColdFusion is a simple language to learn and use, primarily because it employs a tag-based syntax similar to HTML (tags with attributes/values). This was deemed advantageous for the Library because many librarians have experience with tag-based languages and so might feel more comfortable with ColdFusion's code. ColdFusion's syntax makes it possible to develop and deploy applications rapidly with a minimum of programming experience.

- ColdFusion's ability to interact with various relational database management systems, particularly Microsoft's SQL Server 2005. ColdFusion has a native capacity to communicate with a variety of relational database management systems (Oracle, SQL Server, MySQL, Access, and others). Thus the Library felt confident in purchasing a license to Microsoft's SQL Server 2005 to serve as the RDBMS for external Web site content. Concern that the application server would not be able to communicate with it or that it would necessitate any additional add-ons was minimal.

- ColdFusion's support for Multi-Tiered Application Development Architecture. A multi-tiered, or an n-tier, application is an application framework that is broken into different layers, each responsible for part of the complete application. The fundamental architectural core is the use of ColdFusion Components. ColdFusion Components (or CFCs) encapsulate code (functions) into logical units, allowing for code reuse throughout the entire site. This architecture is similar to C function libraries. These code functions are all placed into a separate file (.cfc extension) and can be called up by any page in the site. CFCs can even be called up from other Web sites if need be. This capability allows for the separation of function from data presentation.[24]

- Staff experience and support for ColdFusion. The Library employed staff who had extensive experience with ColdFusion and who could provide a level of support not attainable with the other available products.

- In addition to the use of application server technology, a site requirement set early on in the redesign phase was that the W3C's Cascading Style Sheets (CSS) specification should be adhered to throughout the entire site for all styling of markup elements. In addition, no inline styling of markup would be accepted. All styling would be placed in a separate .css file. Placing CSS styles in a separate file makes the Library's Web pages load faster for users accessing the site on a dial-up connection (less inline markup). Separating presentational styling from its content is vital because it makes the Web site

  - more flexible—users may access the site with PDAs and different browsers;
  - more easily maintainable—style changes happen globally instead of on a per-page basis; and
  - more accessible—users may access the site with screen readers.

    In addition, the ability of CSS to restrict any kind of style sheet to a specific medium allows the Library to implement a site-wide, print-specific style sheet. This eliminated the need to create "printer-friendly" versions for each page. This print style sheet removes parts of each page (navigational bars, logos, etc.) that the user does not typically want to print. Instead of creating totally different markup structures, one for screen and another for print, the Library has created a more efficient site.

The "Database of Databases"

A key feature of the newly revamped Web site is the "database of [subscribed] databases." This is a locally developed database, each record containing title, provider, contents, and description information for all of the Library's subscription databases. Content of the database of databases is handled through a password-protected, Web-based administrative application that allows a designated administrator to create, read, update, and/or delete records (CRUD functions). Changes to the database occur in real time, so the updated information is immediately available on the Library's Web site. This database is periodically indexed using an indexing software system that comes prepackaged with ColdFusion. The indexing system allows users to perform keyword searches across the entire database. Users can also browse alphabetically and retrieve a complete listing of all database records.

One of the challenges of a heavily visited Web site is to make it appear fresh and new every time it is accessed. The "Featured Resource" section of the HAM–TMC Library Home Page randomly selects and displays a record from the database list, creating an element of new content for each visit or browser refresh. In addition, the print style sheet has been formatted to remove extraneous information (side bar navigation, logos, etc.) so users can print a database's description on its own. This has eliminated the need for reference staff to create separate database-specific handouts for their classes. Staff can now navigate to the database application and print out the database information they need directly from the Web site, as-is.

Federated Searching of E-Journals, the Database of Databases, and E-Books

The current application for federated searching of e-journals, the database of subscription databases, and e-books allows users to search the Library's e-journal collection, the database of databases, and the e-book database either simultaneously or individually. The interface to the application provides users with a simple drop-down menu: (1) Database, E-Journal & E-Book, (2) Database only, (3) E-Journal only, and (4) E-Book only. The search box is located directly below the menu. When a search is submitted, the application completes a simple CASE statement check against the drop-down option value and executes code based on the value provided. Content for the e-journals database is indirectly provided by Serials Solutions®. The e-journal data are exported from the vendor on a schedule and imported into the Library's local e-journal database through Microsoft's SQL Server 2005 Integration Services (SSIS) application platform.[25] Because the vendor's e-journals "data on demand" feature brings e-journal data to the Library in Excel format, an SSIS package has been developed to map Excel's columns directly to a table in the e-journals database, using an OLE DB connection. The current process of exporting e-journals data from the vendor is manual—a staff member must go to the vendor's Web site and retrieve the data. The Library hopes to be able to automate this process in the future. The import/export process for the e-books data mirrors that of the e-journals data import/export process.

In addition, the Library added a static RSS 2.0 (Really Simple Syndication) XML file containing URLs of the Library's most critical online resources. These resources include the Library's OPAC; the E-Journals Search Form; the database of databases Web page; and pages containing general information about the Library's hours, latest class schedule, and contact information. This added feature allows HAM–TMC Library users to subscribe to this XML file's content through a "feed reader" or "aggregator" and receive information without having to connect to the Library's Web site.

In July 2007 the Library added a blog to its external Web site. The blog is divided into several main subject categories—News, E-Resources Alerts, and Scholarly Communications—with links to personnel responsible for adding content to their designated subject(s). Content is added through a Web-based interface, which allows the staff content providers to add their entries while offsite. When content is added, it is immediately available for consumption via direct access of the blog URL, viewing the entry link on the Library's home page, or subscribing to the Library's blog. These delivery content mechanisms allow the Library greater flexibility and coverage in delivering content. It is no longer enough to provide content for users and hope they will visit the Library's Web site; now the Library can deliver content directly to them.

Part IV: Conclusion

It is now commonplace to observe that the Internet has brought about global, revolutionary changes. Information of all kinds, and in myriad formats, is available on a scale almost unimaginable just twenty years ago. Libraries traditionally have provided access to chiefly print resources, but the possibilities inherent in the digitization of information of all kinds radically expands the parameters of a library's collections. Those collections are no longer limited to physical items that the library actually owns and stores within its walls. Technology has made it possible for libraries to extend their collections by providing their users with access to proprietary databases, full-text electronic books and journals, and documents residing on servers around the world. The key issue here is how a library guides its users in finding these resources and makes them aware of their existence.

During the past two decades the HAM–TMC Library has evolved from a print-based library to an ever more digital one. Technical services personnel have always acquired, cataloged, and processed resources, and to a certain extent maintained those resources. But as format has changed, so have the roles and scope of technical services staff. The Collections Management Department of the Library has reenvisioned its role in the delivery of content to its users. Above and beyond assigning appropriate subject headings and classification numbers to books or negotiating licenses for access to databases or electronic journals, Collection Management staff members are actively engaged in building new and innovative pathways to resources for the Library's users.

The redesign of the Library's Web site has accomplished the first step in this direction. (See figure 3.5, p. 36.) The new site makes the Library's many resources more easily available, but at present these resources are split among a number of information silos. Plans are in progress to develop a simple way for users to search these disparate silos simultaneously and to present search results in an authoritative and useful manner. The task of providing efficient and effective delivery of content to users is unending and ever-evolving. The Collections Department believes it has made important progress in the right direction, but the rapid advance of technological change means that staff must continue to move forward as swiftly as possible and recognize the opportunities presented by new technologies as they appear.

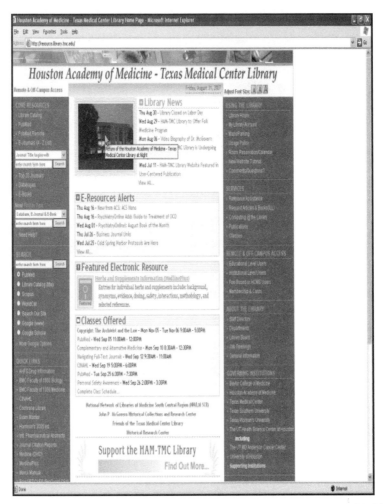

Figure 3.5. Current HAM–TMC Library Web Site Screenshot, August 31, 2007.

Endnotes

1. Baylor College of Medicine and The University of Texas Medical School at Houston.

2. The University of Texas Nursing School at Houston, Texas Woman's University College of Nursing, and Prairie View A&M University College of Nursing.

3. For a full list of the Library's supporting institutions, consult www.library.tmc.edu/about/supinst.cfm.

4. Two of the authors of this article (James and Sanders) have been members of the Technical Services Division in its various configurations for much of the past two decades.

5. Obviously this is a gross understatement of the work involved, but it suffices to make the point.

6. Now the technology coordinator.

7. The Library's fiscal year runs from September 1 through August 31.

8. Houston Academy of Medicine–Texas Medical Center Library Annual Report, 1983–1984, pp. [2–3, 10–13].

9. HAM–TMC Library Annual Report, 1986–1987, p. 4.

10. Ibid. The card catalog was finally dismantled during FY 1988–1989; see HAM–TMC Library Annual Report, 1988–1989, p. 2.

11. HAM–TMC Library Annual Report, 1993, p. 5.

12. Ibid., p. 10.

13. HAM–TMC Library Annual Report, 1993–1994, pp. [4–5].

14. Ibid.

15. By 1999 both the director of cataloging and the assistant executive director for collections and technical services had left, and what had been a division now became the Collections Management Department, overseen by the associate director of collections management, with a staff of 1.5 FTE librarians and 5 FTE paraprofessionals.

16. HAM–TMC Library Annual Report, 1994–1995, p. [7].

17. HAM–TMC Library Annual Report, 2002–2003, p. 4.

18. HAM–TMC Library Annual Report, 2003–2004, p. 2.

19. HAM–TMC Library Biennium Report: Services 2001–2002/2000–2001, p. 6.

20. The advent of a new executive director in FY 1996–1997 brought with it a number of title changes; the head of technical services was now designated as associate director of collections management.

21. The primary responsibilities of the staff member who serve as check-in backup are monographs processing and copy cataloging.

22. Today there are many application servers available on the market, the main ones being Microsoft's ASP.NET, PHP, Ruby on Rails, Java Server Pages (JSP), and Adobe's ColdFusion.

23. This in turn eliminated the possibility of the Library's using Microsoft's ASP.NET.

24. Because of ColdFusion Components' very strict and rigid format and their ability to house collections of similar functions, it was decided earlier on to use CFCs exclusively for all database interaction throughout the Web site. This decision allows for code that is generally very easy to follow and troubleshoot. Creating code that can easily be debugged was an important point when weighed against the lack of staff members with Web site development experience.

25. Integration Services is a high-performance data transformation pipeline for moving data between different systems. It is a replacement for SQL Server 2000's Data Transformation Services (DTS).

4

Technical Services Reorganization in Law Libraries: A Survey

Karen A. Nuckolls

Upon arriving recently at a newly created position as head of technical services at a small academic law library, this author found her work cut out for her: change the department's outdated procedures and bring it into the twenty-first century. After all, change is constant—and scary—and everyone is affected differently by it. The very fact that a new supervisor was coming into a new position to make changes was no doubt upsetting to the staff. Over the years, those who supervise have learned that among library staffs there are those who find change unsettling, those who are intimidated by change, and those who are resistant to change. Arriving at a new job, the challenges are twofold: how to find acceptance and how to unite diverse types. Many can relate to some aspects of this task.

Because the library had been chronically understaffed, the technical services staff had not had a great deal of individual supervision. The first priority was to develop a plan that would build an acquaintance with them and their daily routines, and that would build a relationship within the department. During the first month on the job, three areas were singled out that would more than likely change: staff, procedures, and personal growth—of both the supervisor and her staff.

To begin, one-on-one meetings were scheduled with staff members, during which they were observed at their jobs and any problems or concerns were discussed. In addition, each person was invited to meet with the new supervisor to discuss privately anything he or she felt should be addressed. The tradition of having weekly meetings within the department was begun, and all staff had a chance to give reports on their respective areas. This was important in generating a good team spirit. Using a prepared chart, each staff member was asked to fill in his or her responsibilities, so that duplicate procedures could be identified within each area and weaknesses assessed that could be resolved in the redevelopment of the department.

One project that truly tested newly developed relationships was the reassignment of offices. Plans had been underway for several months to redesign the Technical Services Department. When the supervisor arrived, she shared the public services librarian's office because there wasn't any space for her in Technical Services, which shared two rooms. Because one room was larger than the other, the two Acquisitions Department staff members were switched into the smaller room, and the supervisor joined the Serials Department staff in the larger room. Instead of dreading this change, the staff became fully engaged in the process. A time line was handed out, and on a weekly—and sometimes daily—basis, discussions took place about whether to discard or relocate items, preferences for new chairs, and the configuration of privacy areas. By introducing these topics early on and answering questions whenever they came up, as well as assigning parts of the project to each staff member, the change took place with everyone working for it, instead of against it. It gave the staff a renewed focus on their jobs in the year ahead. They learned that they could tackle large projects and survive, and the process brought technical services personnel together in an improved working relationship.

If change is scary because it is unknown and sometimes uncontrolled, it is possible to create a "safety net" for staff by giving them the ability to participate in the decisions that affect them. Planning, communicating, and involving staff members in all decisions develops methods of working with change instead of against it. Personalities do not change, so it was not possible to create entirely new people; however, there was definitely an increased willingness on the part of the staff to be open to new ideas and methods.[1]

The reorganization described above is only one example of a law library technical services reorganization, and it won't be the last. In a few years there will be a new building to move into, and the process will begin again. Space issues, new staff, retiring staff, promotions, new directors, new media creating new skills—all these and more can provide the impetus to reorganize and redevelop workflow.

A law library may be a special or branch library on campus or a one-person operation in a law firm or courthouse. On an academic campus it is usually smaller than the main library, but its problems are identical as far as staffing and reorganization. A plethora of e-mails, listserv threads, and articles have dealt with technical services, and library, reorganization. One of the factors contributing to this study was the news that the University of Michigan law library had "done away with" its technical services department upon the departure of its department head. This caused a flurry of listserv traffic, mostly from law technical services departments across the country. The library structure that ensued at Michigan was a shifting and combining of functions among other department heads in the library. The director was very excited by this departure from the norm of technical services organization. She listed several important projects that her newly organized staff were implementing: reclassifying "all 25 miles" of books into LC classification, revamping the Web site and creating a new Web site about the history of the law school in anticipation of its fiftieth anniversary, planning for revising all authority records, eliminating all backlogs of materials that needed processing, binding all the serials that had not been bound but were in the stacks, and planning for "Googling" their entire collection starting in summer 2010. The director stated that "this is evidence that with imaginative rethinking, a library really can do more with fewer people."[2]

At Stanford University's law library, there was minimal reorganization of the technical services functions when the position of head of technical services was eliminated. The newly created position of deputy director directly supervises five junior librarians (including reference and technical services functions), and the library director directly supervises three senior librarians. Most policy making is accomplished in a group setting of all professional staff. Technical services staffing remains the same: a catalog librarian and cataloging staff; an acquisitions librarian and staff; and an e-resources/serials librarian with a staff that includes bindery, government documents, and serials. All staff moved into new quarters after working in small, temporary quarters, and now work out problems together, "since as a group we understand what needs to be done." Staff performing technical services tasks sit at workstations adjacent to access services staff.[3]

Even more libraries have to rethink their staffing and organization as e-resources increase their presence in libraries. Far from needing fewer staff members, libraries are finding that additional staffing is needed to handle the new duties of licensing negotiation and database selection and, possibly, print deselection. E-mail messages appear from law technical services departments and public services departments on listservs, asking who is withdrawing print copies of titles appearing in electronic form.

The Survey and Department Size

With the obvious interest being generated, a survey was sent out to law librarians about these issues over various listservs, including law-related, AUTOCAT, and technical services variations. The survey received 571 visits, and of these 165 filled out the survey partially, while 21 filled it out entirely. (These included those who left their contact information at the end of the survey.) Sixty-three percent of the survey was filled out by academic law librarians; 14 percent were law firm librarians; 2 percent were specialized (cataloging outsource agency for twenty law firms, an independent law librarian, and a bar association); and "other" (22 percent) consisted of court, county, and government law librarians. So the group was a varied one.

When asked, "What is the size of your library?," 50 percent answered that they had between 100,000 and 500,000 items, indicating a strong academic showing. Major law libraries with over 500,000 items accounted for 24 percent, and there was a strong showing from smaller law libraries (firm, court, government) at 24 percent. The number of staff (11–20) generated 45 percent, while "10 or less" accounted for 31 percent. In keeping with the larger academic presence, 24 percent answered that they had 21 or more staff members in their libraries. When asked the same question about their technical services departments, however, the number with "10 or less" increased to 88 percent. Again, this could reflect just about all of those who answered: only 12 percent had 11 staff members or more in their technical services departments.

Position in the Library

Directors, department heads, and librarians accounted for the majority of survey responses. Associate/assistant irectors accounted for 15 percent.

Multigenerational?

A growing topic of interest among librarians, as evidenced by surveying conference topics, is the increasing age diversity within libraries, and technical services is no exception. The choices were divided among four generations:

Silents: (born 1945 or earlier)

Baby Boomers (1946–1964)

Gen X (1965–1980)

Millennials (1980–2000)

Not surprisingly, the majority of staff in law libraries consisted of a mixture, with Baby Boomers and Gen Xers predominating. Silents (19 percent) and Millennials (28 percent) followed. The age of staff can have a profound effect on library operations, especially in the twenty-first century. With Baby Boomers beginning to retire, libraries need to depend on Gen Xers and Millennials for immediate, future staffing.

Issues Affecting Reorganization

Retirements account for the majority of staff reorganization in technical services. With technology continuing to change functions, most libraries reorganize every time there is a change in staffing or technology. Technical Services continue to see staff shrinkage. Either a position simply disappears, or it is shifted to Public Services. "Functional" is the major reason that technical services departments are reorganized. Forty-four percent replied that staff reduction or increase accounted for their reorganization. With 36 percent replying "N/A," there are obviously a multitude of other issues that remain undiscovered. The library director made the reorganization decision among 11 percent of respondents; physical (new or renovated building) and change in mission accounted for 14 percent.

Promoting Good Working Relationships

A question about relationships at work was included, because they can be absolutely critical to the administration of a library. As indicated previously, it is important for staff to "buy in" to change to ensure a smooth transition. Here is a summary of responses to this question:

Hold weekly meetings: 8 percent

Use team approach: 42 percent

Have good peer-to-peer relationships: 55 percent

Revise procedures as needed: 52 percent

Have a good relationship with Public Services: 45 percent

All of the above: 27 percent

These percentages show that good working relationships with peers and Public Services fall into the "critical" category. A team approach promotes good relationships within Technical Services. Revising procedures as soon as possible promotes positive workflow and smooth transitions.

Many responded that their library or technical services departments hold monthly or regular meetings. Some hold monthly departmental meetings and biweekly management meetings. Some sponsor a retreat in addition to monthly meetings. Circuit court librarians find it difficult to meet regularly. Some have an e-list for catalogers and one for clients. Law firms with multistate branches communicate regularly via e-mail and hold an annual meeting. Two of the most interesting comments were: "Honest, respect, fair, communication," and "Work around the unchangeables, appreciate gems."

Smaller law libraries are "too small to have bad relationships." Others use a strategic plan to clarify goals. Still others are one-person libraries, so he or she has to do it all! And others answer that they have "very little of the above [good working relationships]; top down management."

Reason for Your Technical Services Reorganization

There were interesting responses to this question, some expected: experienced growth; new head/supervisor; retirements; new procedures; planning for new building; promotions; new ILS, e-resources; modernized with new technical services head; improved services. Some departments simply "evolved over several years." One technical services department did not exist before 2003! One department "applied creativity to make jobs more interesting." One wanted to "raise standards, usability, [and] cost savings." Within one department, "people traded positions for [a] better fit." Still, there were others who answered that they were in "dire need of such reorganization," and had had "no evaluation of work flow for [the] last 15–20 years."

The Role of E-Resources, Metadata, and Digital in Technical Services Change

The unsurprising answer to this question was: Not much. Most academic law libraries have consortial agreements on campus with other libraries for sharing databases, online catalogs, ERMs, and the like. Although they were perhaps among the first libraries to use databases (LexisNexis, WestLaw), there is still quite a bit of dependence on print resources, especially for the older materials. Many law resources are still easier to use on paper, although some are easier to use online. Law libraries will continue to rely on both the printed, and electronic, word.

Law libraries and law schools rely heavily on the American Bar Association annual statistics, always fun to fill out. During the survey, respondents indicated that they also fill out in-house statistics (52 percent), which are probably used for the ABA (38 percent) survey.

Planning a Reorganization

To the question, "How was your reorganization planned?," more than 37 percent answered that the library director or dean planned it, and 24 percent answered that it was the department head. There were a few committees and outside consultants. Replies included "everybody together"; "all-staff effort led by Dept. Head"; "it evolved over several years"; "by the people who do the TS work"; "Asst. Dir. For TS with Cataloger and TS staff input"; "Section heads, we have no department head"; "initially by the director, subsequently with input"; and then, "We haven't reorganized Technical Services-won't"; and "It happened. There was no plan."

Reorganization Structures

Although there are many different kinds of reorganization templates, five basic kinds were included in the survey:

Hierarchical (5-tier): Director/Dean, Assoc./Assist. Director/Dean, Dept. Heads, Section Heads, Staff

Hierarchical (4-tier): Director/Dean, Dept. Heads, Section Heads, Staff

Hierarchical (3-tier): Director/Dean, Assoc./Assist. Director/Dean(s), Staff

Flattened: Director/Dean, Assoc./Assist. Director/Dean(s), Staff

Flattened: Director/Dean, Area Librarians (by function), Staff

When asked about what structure their library/technical services department organized *from*, the answers were split primarily among the 3-tier (18 percent), 4-tier (13 percent), and flattened with area librarians (11 percent). The complete library was included here in order to gain additional comments. One library reorganized from a management committee, library heads, and IT heads. Another had a technical services librarian in acquisitions, a cataloger, and a clerk. Still another had central processing spread across four branches. "We reorganized departments within tech services." One position changed from a manager who cataloged to an assistant librarian who did the cataloging.

The replies were just as varied when asked about the structure their library/technical services department organized *to*. One library still consisted of a 4-tier structure, but created new units and section heads. Other comments were "centralization yet little official hierarchical change"; "cataloguers working at a distance"; "same structure just reassigned duties"; "director, everyone else (initially)"; "Acquisitions was removed from Technical Services"; "distance management"; "separated serials from acquisitions"; and "reorg. people, policies and flow, not structure." Many departments just reassigned staff to different functions or areas, some separated technical services functions from the department, and some clearly had moved their cataloging, possibly to another building.

Many branch libraries on a campus face the real possibility of consolidating their technical services at the main library. This can present some difficulties in the law library because of to the nature of the materials used by law students, faculty, and lawyers. "Continuing resources," which consist of successive and integrating resources, make up a large part of the workflow in a law technical services department and have an impact in all areas of the department. It is critical to get these materials out to patrons, whether it is filing loose-leafs or pocket parts or pulling one volume of the United States Code Annotated and replacing it with five volumes. Being separated physically from the law library can create detrimental delays in getting updated materials onto the shelves.

Has Your Position Changed? What Factors Influenced That Change?

This question only asked for comments, and there were several responses. Many moved up from a librarian position to head of technical services; many moved up to a librarian position upon receiving the MLS. Some were promoted from technical services to deputy director. The departure of one acquisitions librarian (not replaced) led to a reassignment of many units and reporting structures. Another acquisitions retirement resulted in a cataloger taking on the acquisitions role. This was another way of looking at it: "New Executive Director reorganized the library into three units: Library Operations; Technology Services; Financial Services. He is an attorney, not a librarian."

One newly minted librarian stepped into a void left by a departure in technical services. She is being used to "test out" whether the library needs another librarian in technical services. She is the acting metadata librarian and oversees most of the e-resource work (acquisition, accounting, cataloging, ERM, maintenance). Another librarian began her position, but it immediately changed because she had a BA in computer network administration. A cataloger was responsible for most of technical services duties except acquisitions. Systems was then added to her duties, and supervision of public technicians was removed.

One law librarian leads a large team which, besides technical services work, is responsible for adding content to the library's Web product, as well as indexing records and briefs before digitizing them. Others have additional duties assigned with automation, such as e-resources cataloging and batch loading MARC records.

Summation

This survey highlighted the similarities between law librarians and other librarians. Although some of the material they handle is quite different, the problems they encounter on a daily basis are essentially the same. The challenges law librarians deal with are basically the same. The staffing structures, whether in a law firm, county court, or academic setting, undergo the same changes for the same reasons.

A mandate comes down from the director. Technical services staff meet to discuss a new building area. There are reassignment of functions, retirements, and new staff. We all work through the changes to ensure that our operations continue. And they will continue throughout (at least) the twenty-first century .

Endnotes

1. Karen A. Nuckolls, "Change in a Small Law Library: How We Moved Our Department into the 21st Century,"*Information Outlook* 9, no. 4 (April 2005): 23–24.

2. Margaret A. Leary, "Re: Reorganization," e-mail message, October 24, 2007.

3. Kathy Winzer, "RE: End of TS? Stanford's Experience," ts-sis@aallnet.org, September 11, 2007.

Appendix to Chapter 4: Survey

Technical Services Reorganization in Law Libraries

This survey concerns law libraries in particular, whether academic, firm, or specialized.

Your answers will remain anonymous if you wish.

Thanks for your participation.

---

1. Please indicate the type of library in which you work.
   ☐ Academic (Law School)
   ☐ Firm
   ☐ Private/specialized
   ☐ N/A
   ☐ Other, please specify: _____

---

2. What is the size of your library?
   ☐ Under 100,000 items
   ☐ 100,000–500,000 items
   ☐ Over 500,000 items
   ☐ N/A
   ☐ Other, please specify: _____

---

3. What is the number of staff (librarians and paraprofessionals) in your library?
   ☐ 10 or less
   ☐ 11–20
   ☐ 21–50
   ☐ Over 50
   ☐ N/A
   ☐ Additional comments: _____

4. What is the size of your library's Technical Services Department (or the number of library staff who deal with technical services issues)?

☐ 10 or less

☐ 11–20

☐ 21–50

☐ Over 50

☐ N/A

☐ Additional comments: _____

5. Which most clearly describes your position in your library?

☐ Director/Dean

☐ Associate/Assistant Director/Dean

☐ Department Head

☐ Section Head

☐ Supervisor

☐ Librarian

☐ Paraprofessional

☐ N/A

☐ Other, please specify: _____

6. Describe your Technical Services Department (or equivalent). How multigenerational is it?

☐ Silents (Born in 1945 or earlier)

☐ Baby Boomers (1946–1964)

☐ Gen X (1965–1980)

☐ Millennials (1980–2000)

☐ N/A

☐ Other, please specify: _____

7. In what ways do you promote good working relationships?

☐ Hold weekly meetings

☐ Use team approach

☐ Good peer-to-peer relationships

☐ Revise procedures as needed

☐ Have a good relationship with Public Services

☐ All of the above

☐ N/A

☐ Additional comments: _____

8. What was the reason for your Technical Services reorganization?

☐ New Director/Dean

☐ Physical (new building/renovation)

☐ Functional (staff reduction/increase, e-resources)

☐ Change in mission

☐ N/A

☐ Other, please specify: _____

9. If electronic resources (e-journals, databases, digital, etc.) were the reason for your reorganization, what effect have they had on technical services functions? (5 = most effect)

	1	2	3	4	5
Training	☐	☐	☐	☐	☐
Outsourcing	☐	☐	☐	☐	☐
Maintain own IT Department	☐	☐	☐	☐	☐
Maintain own website, ERMs	☐	☐	☐	☐	☐
N/A	☐	☐	☐	☐	☐

10. What kinds of statistics do you keep?

☐ ABA

☐ ARL

☐ Inhouse

☐ All of the above

☐ N/A

☐ Other, please specify: _____

11. How was your reorganization planned?

☐ Director/Dean

☐ Department Head(s)

☐ Library Committee

☐ Technical Services Committee

☐ Outside Consultant

☐ N/A

☐ Other, please specify: _____

12. What kind of structure did you reorganize from?

☐ Hierarchical (5-tier) Director/Dean, Assoc./Assist. Dean, Dept. Heads, Section Heads, Staff

☐ Hierarchical (4-tier) Director/Dean, Dept. Heads, Section Heads, Staff

☐ Hierarchical (3-tier) Director/Dean, Dept. Heads, Staff

☐ Flattened: Director/Dean, Assoc./Assist. Director/Dean(s), Staff

☐ Flattened: Director/Dean, Area Librarians (by function), Staff

☐ N/A

☐ Other, please specify: _____

13. What kind of structure did you reorganize to?

☐ Hierarchical (5-tier) Director/Dean, Assoc./Assist. Director/Dean, Dept. Heads, Section Heads, Staff

☐ Hierarchical (4-tier) Director/Dean, Dept. Heads, Section Heads, Staff

☐ Hierarchical (3-tier) Director/Dean, Dept. Heads, Staff

☐ Flattened: Director/Dean, Assoc./Assist. Director/Dean(s), Staff

☐ Flattened: Director/Dean, Area Librarians (by function), Staff

☐ N/A

☐ Other, please specify: _____

14. If your position has changed, what factors influenced that change? Please describe.

_____

_____

_____

_____

_____

_____

15. May I contact you to follow up on your answers?

☐ Yes   ☐ No

16. If you answered "yes," please enter your name and contact information:

Last Name: _____

First Name: _____

Email address: _____

Phone:_____

5

Creative Ideas in Staffing: Shared Responsibilities, Hybrid Positions, and Taking Full Advantage of the Connections Between Public and Technical Services

Laurie Phillips

The debate over catalogers working at the reference desk is puzzling—inevitably, the us versus them mentality comes out in full force. Catalogers ask, "Why should we have to take ourselves away from our 'real' work? Isn't that work valued? Why don't reference librarians have to do cataloging in return?" The underlying message is that the reference librarians wouldn't be qualified to do technical services work anyway. The truth is, unless one is at a large research or public library, positions are not specialized enough for librarians to be purely reference librarians. No one can spend forty hours per week at the reference desk and still enjoy the job. The pace is too frenetic, and there is little time to accomplish anything else while tethered to a public desk. This means that everyone who works in the library—technical services librarians and staff or public services librarians and staff—has work that takes place behind the scenes, off of the public desk. So why shouldn't the technical services librarian participate in face-to-face service to users? And shouldn't this model be extended to include support staff as well? Creating a better mix of responsibilities builds flexibility, knowledge, portability of skills, and a bigger picture view of the library and its goals. Working directly with users brings the perspective of the user to the behind-the-scenes work. Can users interpret serials holdings in the catalog? Can information generated by the link resolver inform collection development? Can new connections in the workflow be seen and utilized?

In addition, library users are provided better services by bringing a group of people together at the front desk with a mix of knowledge and skills who can bring a synergy to the work that would not happen in any other way. The J. Edgar & Louise S. Monroe Library at Loyola University New Orleans now employs a one-desk model for circulation, reference, and basic technology support services. Technical services and public services librarians and staff and student workers are working together at one desk, providing a myriad of services to the end user. As Diane Zabel pointed out in 2005, the "consolidation of service points is closely tied to another important trend: the integration of public and technical services . . . . The rationale is that patrons do not care who is staffing the desk; they just want service."[1] By providing a mix of expertise at the desk, this library is able to provide a higher level of service without sending the user all over the library for help.

For several years, technical services librarians at the Monroe Library helped out at the reference desk. What began as filling in when the public services division was short a librarian, for various reasons became a permanent part of the jobs of the technical services librarians. In fact, when a new technical services librarian was hired whose duties included systems, she chose to take additional hours at the circulation desk to learn more about user records and the circulation functions in the system. Her experience was invaluable, both to learning her job and to the library, and made her the perfect librarian to take responsibility for developing training for staff and librarians when the reference and circulation desks merged. After Hurricane Katrina, when Loyola University had to downsize staff, the library was fortunate to lose only those positions to which the person in them did not return. Unfortunately, two of those positions were among the circulation staff, making staffing and scheduling challenging at best. The library is open 115 hours per week and has not reduced hours since the staff reductions. Student satisfaction and retention are crucial in this challenging time of rebuilding. In the spring semester of 2006, technical services staff volunteered to assume some key daytime hours at the circulation desk, covering busy lunch times and some afternoon hours. Now that they are more experienced and well trained, they also readily volunteer to fill in on evenings and weekends when public services staff are sick or on vacation. Technical services staff know that the public services staff have less flexibility to take time off, so they have been generous in helping to accommodate the leave requests of their colleagues. The temporary volunteer situation has now become a fully integrated, permanent part of the jobs of the technical services staff.

Technical services staff have expressed positive feedback about their work at the desk. They like being able to step away from the detailed, concentrated, solitary work that they do, and step out into the busy, bustling world of the public services desk. They enjoy bringing the expertise of their jobs to direct service to the user. A cataloger can add a brief record on the spot for an item not found in the catalog (and is more able to determine if there is already a record in the catalog) and get the item immediately to the user. In fact, through the magic of remote desktop software, a cataloger can even do on-the-spot, retrospective conversion after the initial transaction is completed. When a student casually mentions that he is checking to see if the library owns a particular movie on DVD, the librarian involved with collection development is more likely to point the student to the form where new materials can be requested than to say, "No, we don't own that."

The librarian or support staff person with cataloging or systems responsibilities brings a wealth of experience and skills to the user. Catalogers and systems administrators know the MARC record and indexing better than anyone else. Catalogers are the ones who put the information into the catalog and know better how to retrieve it. They understand the structure of subject headings and how they are applied. They are also very involved in decisions about indexing and how the catalog works for searching. For example, in the Monroe Library's online catalog, the contents note is indexed in both the title and author indexes, for retrieval of chapter titles and authors. The average public services staff member will not be aware of all the intricacies of storage and retrieval of information. Catalogers tend to have more foreign language expertise, which is very helpful in working with music or foreign films, where the title that pops up in a brief display may be the title in the original language. The staff or librarians with responsibility for systems have a knowledge of the data structure of the integrated library system and technology trouble-shooting skills that can be very useful at a public desk that supports both circulation of materials and patrons using library-owned hardware and software, in addition to courseware and user-owned hardware and software. As Sandy Folsom noted, "When a cataloging background is combined with a public services position, the result can be a very potent force for bringing high quality assistance to patrons."[2] In addition, technical services librarians and staff bring a variety of subject expertise to their work at the front desk. In 2003 the Monroe Library closed its only branch library, the music library, and moved the music collection to the main library. By doing so, music library services went from two staff members with music expertise to seven, adding in those in the main library with music degrees or expertise. Two of the technical services librarians have advanced degrees in music, and having them at the front desk on a regular basis, along with the actual music librarian and former music library staff member, allows for better experiences at the main library for users who need help with music materials. This is especially true when dealing with music reserves, which can be large, difficult to manage, and challenging in terms of finding the correct item for the user.

Amy L. Carver pointed out that, "Communication and sharing expertise are critical to achieving the fundamental mission of the library and providing patrons access to information and library materials. Open lines of communication between catalogers and reference librarians are essential to capitalize fully on this mission."[3] This is true not only for catalogers and reference librarians, but for public and technical services staff as well. One issue discovered at the Monroe Library, in the midst of training for implementation of the one-desk model, was that public services staff did not have a good sense of the workflow and possibilities for services emanating from technical services, such as rush purchase, rush cataloging, and helping users find items that seem to be missing. The public services staff knew to fill out the form to report missing items so that staff could search for them, but were not carrying the process further to look for the item at another library where the user could borrow it, or to expedite the process of purchasing another copy if the item were not found. Reference librarians routinely called catalogers to request rush cataloging for users, but other public services staff were more likely to place a hold in the catalog for a rush request to be filled the next day. With technical services staff and librarians working together with public services staff, many of those miscommunications have been resolved. In fact, one of the library's strategic initiatives for 2008 was to smooth communication and workflow between back-of-the-house work and the front desk. Staff who work on the processes behind the scenes are working to flowchart the processes to clarify them for themselves first, which will ensure that communication takes place with all of those librarians and staff who work at the front desk. In the meantime, because different types of staff are all working together, misconceptions can be corrected as they come to light. If there are problems with an item, such as the on-order or in-process copy still showing after an item is cataloged, the cataloger working at the desk is more likely to come across it and fix it if he or she is working directly with users at the desk. Steve Hardlin describes this very situation, in which a library user would report a problem in the catalog (a call number not displaying properly), and he could fix it on the spot.[4] If a cataloging or acquisitions staff member is helping a user with an item that is on order, he or she might check the ILS to determine when the order was placed, better informing the user's decision to place a hold on it. Remote desktop allows use of all the tools that reside on office computers while working at the front desk. Increasingly, librarians are choosing to use laptop computers rather than desktops, so work is portable and may be brought to the front desk with them.

In a medium-sized university library like the J. Edgar & Louise S. Monroe Library, all librarians and staff have significant responsibilities in addition to desk hours. Each library faculty member is a liaison to one or more academic departments, meaning that the librarian has a mix of collection development, outreach, and instruction responsibilities in those subject areas. The public services librarians, in addition to serving a number of hours per week at the front desk (called the "Learning Commons Desk"), have responsibility for leading initiatives in outreach, instruction, distance library services, and online services. Technical services librarians have a mix of responsibilities in collection management, cataloging, systems, electronic journal management, and online services. All of the library's teams (Web, information resources, technology, teaching and learning, etc.) include a mix of public and technical services staff and librarians. Obviously, one of the values of teaching in a liaison subject area means that one has direct contact with the students and faculty and can understand the assignments they are undertaking with the library's resources. The Information Resources Team relies heavily on the librarian liaisons for input into decisions about electronic resources and serials subscriptions, but the fact that all of the librarians are teaching and providing reference services means that no one is out of touch with the end user.

The Technical Services Division of the Monroe Library was created in a reorganization in 1998 from three departments: acquisitions, cataloging, and serials. Two positions involving binding (serials and monographs) were combined into one and merged with processing. Two department head positions were dissolved (serials and acquisitions), with one of those librarians (collection development) remaining in Technical Services. Collection development for both serials and monographs was combined into one position, and serials management remains the purview of a support staff member, although work with electronic journal management is done by a technical services librarian. As more journals are moved online and there are fewer print journals to check in, claim, and manage, more of the responsibility for electronic journal management may be moved to the staff position.

The cataloging department originally had two librarians and two staff catalogers. With improvements in automation and desktop computing, cataloging has become much faster. The improved authorization capabilities of the OCLC Connexion client alone have greatly enhanced the speed at which catalogers can work, especially when working with authorities-heavy materials such as sound recordings and media. Much of the library's book cataloging has been outsourced, with two cataloging assistants performing much of the rest of the cataloging and only one professional cataloger remaining (also serving as the associate dean for technical services). The one professional cataloger catalogs those materials that require specialized expertise, such as music, media, and electronic resources. With the use of the OCLC Promptcat service, the book cataloging process is fairly streamlined and only requires a staff member to oversee the process, handled almost entirely by student workers.

The library's catalogers made the decision to no longer edit or proofread full level Library of Congress cataloging. Many catalogers will make the case that Library of Congress records are not perfect, but they are still better than most and certainly not substandard cataloging. Most libraries no longer have the luxury of time or people to spend on obsessively proofreading or upgrading those cataloging records. This means some compromise, of course. Previously, bibliographies classed in LC class Z were reclassed into their subject area. With the move to accepting LC records without editing, those materials would no longer be reclassed. This was a difficult decision to make, because the reclassing made sense and did serve a purpose. Gift books remain the single most difficult group of materials to deal with. Large gift collections of sound recordings have been handled fairly well by downloading cataloging records, placing them in order on shelving by composer and title, then cataloging them as time allows or demand dictates. Gift books often come in large batches, and the Technical Services Division has neither storage space for a backlog nor staff to manage the downloading of records or cataloging. As a result, the library is extremely particular about accepting gift books. They must support the curriculum and be usable by the undergraduate population.

Acquisitions at the Monroe Library is handled by one full-time administrative staff person, supplemented by well-trained student workers who do receiving. Currently, the acquisitions staff member is downloading cataloging records for each title ordered, creating order records in the online system, then submitting them electronically to the vendor using EDI. With a new process under development between Blackwell's (the library's major book vendor) and OCLC, however, it will be possible to receive full cataloging records with order data embedded in them at the time of order. The time savings this new program represents will be huge on the acquisitions end. Using student workers for receiving has had mixed success. The student workers have done a wonderful job, but any attendance problems can derail the workflow, and received materials get piled up during every break period.

Before reorganization, two positions carried partial responsibility for binding—one in acquisitions and one in serials. Those two partial positions were combined into one that also has responsibility for repairs, in-house binding, and overseeing processing. The person in this position is the only one in the current technical services area who does not work at the Learning Commons desk. The most introverted of the staff, although extremely personable, this staff member chooses instead to contribute to public services work in other ways, by searching for missing items in the stacks and serving on the stacks maintenance team.

Serials was its own department and is now essentially handled by one staff member, with considerable support from the collection development librarian and technical services librarian. Managing serials can be frustrating and grueling. The post-Katrina problems with the United States Postal Service made this job one of the most difficult in the library. Just working through the maze of bureaucracy in trying to get serials delivered has been challenging, to say the least. As a result, this staff member, although extremely busy with her serials responsibilities, has taken the most desk hours of the technical services group. She enjoys being able to walk away from the frustrations associated with serials for a couple of hours and work with people. She regularly works on routine tasks from the front desk, like maintaining holdings in the catalog, but it is a welcome break. In addition, student workers at the front desk who work with her are getting a taste of what it takes to maintain the periodicals collection and what all of that information means. Her contribution at the front desk is invaluable and allows her to stay longer in her job without burning out.

Technical services staff all report that they enjoy their public services responsibilities. When they initially volunteered, no one expected that the assignment would become permanent, but staff have seen the need and the transition toward more integration of services and areas. They readily see the connection between the front of the house and the back of the house and are contributing to the development of better processes, procedures, and communication.

At the time of the reorganization, responsibility for maintenance of the integrated library system was under Public Services, and professional positions in technical services were the technical services coordinator, collection development librarian, and a cataloger. Since then an evolution of sorts has taken place. First, systems moved under Technical Services. Where systems responsibilities reside in a library is so often governed by where automation first took root—generally either in circulation or cataloging. In 2001, in an attempt to clarify responsibilities for systems, the dean of librarians and another librarian did a small telephone survey of other libraries with the same integrated library system, to determine how and where systems responsibilities were handled. One library's solution sounded perfect for the Monroe Library—the systems responsibilities were shared by the technical services coordinator and a cataloger. When the systems position (a high-level staff position) was vacated several years ago, the position was changed to a librarian's position to provide more flexibility, but it was filled with a person whose primary responsibility was still systems, with some responsibilities for electronic journal management. In the interim, systems responsibilities were assumed by the new division coordinator, paving the way for a shared model in the future. Now systems responsibilities are shared by a team of three people: the associate dean for technical services, the technical services librarian (whose title is soon to be changed to "Systems and Metadata Initiatives Coordinator"), and the circulation manager. The three people involved meet to form policies; set due dates and expiration dates; work on problem solving; and plan for upgrades, training, and system changes. Each person handles different responsibilities, ranging from managing policies and loading student records to installing new products such as EDI, coordinating beta testing, catalog maintenance, and backups (daily and weekly). The wonderful result of shared responsibility for the online system is that no one person has all of the knowledge. There are three people who can troubleshoot problems at circulation, in technical services, or with things like the Z39.50 server. All calls to client care are funneled through a central e-mail address, where all three people can check progress on problems being dealt with through the online system vendor.

The position that is now associate dean for technical services was the library's first model of the evolution toward hybrid positions. Although hired as a music and media cataloger, the librarian in this position began teaching in the library's instruction program in the early 1990s, when the library first took responsibility for instruction in new technologies such as e-mail and the Web. When the library moved into a new facility and reference services came into higher demand, she began taking regular reference hours when the public services division was short a person for whatever reason (leaves, vacancies, etc.). Over time the position maintained regular reference responsibilities, even when a full complement of public services librarians was in place. This became crucial when the library took on a particularly grueling schedule of digital reference in partnership with another library in the region. Now the associate dean moves seamlessly between the public and technical services arenas, functioning in an administrative role, working as a cataloger (still cataloging sound recordings and media), teaching library instruction, and providing services at the Learning Commons desk. When stepping down to the front desk between meetings or to drop off newly cataloged videos, the associate dean inevitably finds staff or librarians with questions or work that can be accomplished right there. The associate dean recently took responsibility for library reserves, recognizing that the behind-the-scenes work of reserves in bringing materials to the user is not all that different from acquisitions and cataloging. In this work, expertise with workflow and problem solving is brought to the reserves arena, and new connections are being developed with collection development. Faculty are sent reserves use statistics at the end of each semester, and regular communication is taking place regarding the processing of electronic reserves. Poor quality personal VHS copies, once placed on reserve, are now being replaced with library-owned DVDs. Although there are some challenges in taking oversight responsibility in an area where the staff do not report to the team leader, significant improvements have taken place in the area of reserves in the past academic year.

When the previous ILS coordinator left, the position was completely re-evaluated, and the Technical Services Division thought that hiring another professional cataloger might be important. The position would, of course, still have varied responsibilities, including shared responsibility for the ILS and liaison responsibilities that include collection development and teaching. In the end, the person hired had a strong cataloging background but currently does no cataloging of physical materials, although she works with metadata describing virtual objects in Special Collections. In fact, she now coordinates all of the post-scanning technical processes associated with digitizing projects in Special Collections. That said, it has been very useful to have someone with a firm background in cataloging, knowledge of the MARC format, and the data structure of catalog records. The attention to detail and the approach to work found in a cataloger are invaluable, but the actual cataloging took a back seat to other more pressing work that a person with that background and skills could accomplish. Although the responsibilities of this position sit primarily in the technical services arena, the public services responsibilities and outlook allow her to see connections between the work in each area. When establishing access to a new electronic journal, she tests the ability of the user to easily get to it and works with the publishers to allow more user-friendly access. She works with the link resolver software and runs reports that inform decisions about serials collection development. The information resources team has chosen to move many journals in focused subject areas (primarily business, nursing, and criminal justice) to online-only, based on information gathered from the link resolver and other resources. She has become involved in work on the Web site that feeds into technical services work, such as developing new Web forms for requests for purchase.

In the end, a cataloger's approach and background was needed, but not an actual cataloger. The library needed someone who could thrive in an environment with varied tasks and responsibilities and see the connections between technical and public services work, using information gathered from one area to inform the other. It takes a well-organized person who likes variety to thrive in this environment. Regular check-ins about priorities and progress are crucial to making this position work. Hybrid positions have existed in libraries for many years, but these "jack of all trades" types of positions often referred to librarians in branch libraries, for example, music librarians who also did music cataloging, such as the position described by Beth Tice.[5] The types of positions evolving in the Monroe library are not subject-oriented, but serving the needs of the whole library. Christine DeZelar-Tiedman discusses tailoring library positions to match individual skills. In this case, the library is making full use of the librarian's skills in both the public and technical services arenas, recognizing the value of someone who can see the big picture of the library's needs.

Although we do not want to overwhelm an individual, we also do not want artificial boundaries to get in the way of making use of skills and expertise in the organization. In fact, a varied position may be more likely to prevent rather than cause burnout. One other important component to making it work is to regularly review the job description, at least annually, to ensure that the job description still reflects the reality of the position's responsibilities, especially as they inevitably evolve, and that the primary responsibilities still reflect the needs of the division and the library. A recent retooling of this position's job description was very useful in redefining the responsibilities and recognizing growth, resulting in a proposal to change the position's title from the generic "Technical Services Librarian" to "Systems and Metadata Initiatives Coordinator." Finding appropriate yet more specific titles for hybrid and varied positions can be very challenging.

As Gail Z. Eckwright and Mary K. Bolin wrote, "To create a hybrid, the library must be able to look beyond the functional organization of services to a more collegial model that is not task-oriented or bureaucratic." This segues perfectly into a discussion of the library's first true hybrid position. With the development of the Learning Commons and moving all services to one desk, the position of circulation coordinator as it stood became obsolete. But the person in that position was and is responsible for many other tasks behind the scenes, including billing for lost materials; setting due dates, expiration dates, and closed dates in the integrated library system; and working with missing and damaged materials. So much of this work involves interaction with collection management, acquisitions, and cataloging, that this person is now serving on the acquisitions/cataloging team. She is doing work in withdrawal of materials that was once done by cataloging staff, using both the integrated library system and OCLC Connexion. The discarded materials never have to be brought to the technical services workroom. As her position evolves, she is reporting almost equally to the associate deans for public and technical services. Because she has worked with both associate deans extensively and well over the years, this transition has worked very smoothly. It takes flexibility and good communication, but both supervisors work with her closely on a regular basis and communicate so often with her and each other that it has not been a problem. As Christine DeZelar-Tiedman wrote, "there is no longer a consensus among library administrators as to what is a public services function and what is a technical services function."[6] There seems to be no reason to pigeonhole functions into positions in one area or another. Off-the-desk work can be related to either area, and responsibilities can be expanded in either direction.

One thing that has greatly aided the Monroe Library's ability to share responsibilities and create hybrid positions is its collaborative organization and team-based structure. If a staff member or librarian is performing work in an area outside of his or her home work team, his or her supervisor gets regular feedback on the work. In the case of a true hybrid, the two supervisors will collaborate on the annual evaluation and development plan and both will give regular feedback. Regular, not just annual, feedback is crucial to everything working smoothly. The supervisor must know about challenges in setting priorities or work responsibilities in any area and must meet regularly with staff to discuss the work, mentor them, and solve problems with them. This works best when there is open communication between the staff member and the supervisor. There must be trust that the staff member will not allow responsibilities in one area to overtake another area. When evening or weekend hours need to be covered, the public services staff is spread thin, so technical services staff are the obvious resource to tap. Technical services staff are encouraged to contribute in this way, always with a discussion regarding the impact on their regular work. Librarians and staff in technical services are juggling many responsibilities, and that includes the head of the division. Staff see the associate dean for technical services moving from desk to classroom to cataloging to administrative meetings, trying not to drop any of the balls, and know that there is mentoring, support, and empathy for their own situations. The acquisitions/cataloging team meets monthly to check in with one another and to share information about projects and issues, and the individuals meet at least monthly with their supervisors to talk about projects and priorities.

Conclusion

All of this is still a work in progress. Its not perfect, but it is working well. Hybrid positions have been an unqualified success. Those librarians and staff at the Monroe Library in hybrid positions feel as if the work is varied, interesting, and integrated, and allows a unique picture of the workings of the whole library. New skills and perspective are brought to public services work, and the experience and information gained from direct contact with students and faculty are brought to bear on work taking place behind the scenes. The one-desk model is new but is quickly showing its value. Bringing together librarians, staff, and students from all over the library to serve users together is providing a wealth of expertise and information to interactions with the library's users. Librarians have more direct contact with faculty on a regular basis and can model good reference skills to the staff and students who previously worked only with circulation and reserves. Technical services staff say that they enjoy working with users and like being able to bring their particular expertise to directly serving users. As the acquisitions coordinator once said, it can be extremely satisfying to check out a book that you personally ordered or rush cataloged for someone. Each person sees the connections between his or her work and what takes place in the rest of the library. That can mean happier, more satisfied staff who are less likely to burn out, and more satisfied library users who are getting excellent service from both the front desk and behind the scenes.

Endnotes

1. Diane Zabel, "Trends in Reference and Public Services Librarianship and the Role of RUSA," *Reference & User Services Quarterly* 45, no. 1 (2005): 9.

2. Sandy L. Folsom, "Out of the Nest: The Cataloger in a Public Services Role," *Library Collections, Acquisitions, & Technical Services* 24 (2000): 67.

3. Amy L. Carver, "We Are All ReferenceLibrarians: Using Communication to Employ a Philosophy of Access for Catalogers," *College & Research Libraries News* 63, no. 3 (2002): 169.

4. Steve Hardlin, "The Servant of Two Masters," *Technicalities* 13, no. 7 (1993): 11.

5. Beth Tice, "Two Hats, One Heart: Confessions of a Split Position Librarian," *Technicalities* 18, no. 7 (1998): 4.

6. Christine DeZelar-Tiedman, "A Perfect Fit: Tailoring Library Positions to Match Individual Skills," *Journal of Library Administration* 29, no. 2 (1999): 30.

6

Making Room for the Future: Facilitating Change through Technical Services Reorganization at Northwestern University Library

Roxanne Sellberg

Introduction

It is an old, oft-repeated story. A new chief executive officer comes to a large academic library. Within a year or so the organizational structure of the library undergoes significant change. Sometimes these library reorganizations have little or no impact on the staff or day-to-day operations of technical services. At other times they result in huge changes to technical services, such as the outsourcing of work formerly performed by resident staff, the movement of "backroom operations" to locations remote from collections and public service points, and the centralization or decentralization of major technical services processes. The technical services impact of Northwestern University's most recent library reorganization promises to fall somewhere in between these extremes. The library reorganization is focused on improving public services and collections and on developing digital infrastructure and services. The changes in administrative structure called for by the library's reorganization can be accomplished without disruption to most technical services operations or trauma for most technical services staff. The restructuring of the library overall, however, has inspired a serious consideration of how technical services staff and activities should be organized for the next few years. By making some organizational changes in anticipation of new technical service challenges and priorities, the library is "making room" for the future.

Organizational Environment

Northwestern University Library (NUL) serves a private university of approximately 17,000 students and 7,000 faculty and staff. The main library, from which the University Library system is administered, is located on the Evanston, Illinois campus. Northwestern's medical and law schools, both on the Chicago campus, are served by separate libraries reporting to the deans of those professional schools. The Northwestern University Press reports to the university librarian (UL) but functions as a separate organization. The University Library stewards collections containing more than 3.8 million volumes and a variety of electronic and other resources. Its collections are particularly rich in material for the study of Africa, transportation, and twentieth-century music. Nearly 300 (full-time equivalent) librarians and other staff work in the University Library system, and NUL's annual expenditures exceed $20 million.

A highlight of NUL's history was the development of the NOTIS library management system, which was implemented by many academic libraries in the 1970s and 1980s. Northwestern has maintained a good reputation in cooperative cataloging programs, invested in a strong preservation program, and was an early implementer of an electronic reserves system. The University Library enjoyed a period of relative stability under the leadership of David Bishop, who was chief executive from 1992 to 2006. This period was marked by active participation in the Committee on Institutional Cooperation (CIC) consortium, a solid record of fund-raising, benign campus relationships, and a series of building renovations. During Bishop's tenure NUL migrated from its homegrown NOTIS system to the Voyager library management system, implemented the SFX and MetaLib systems from Ex Libris, and accomplished a series of digital library projects.

Sarah Pritchard assumed the position of university librarian at Northwestern University in the autumn of 2006. Pritchard was an experienced chief executive officer, having directed the libraries at Smith College and the University of California, Santa Barbara. She started to articulate her vision for Northwestern University Library's future upon her arrival. In common with many large research libraries, she asserted, NUL needed to enhance its support of teaching and research to remain central to the university.

Pritchard envisioned a more flexible organization with collections, programs, and services more closely aligned with the university's evolving curricular and research priorities. She wanted to focus the library organization's attention outward, toward users, toward donors, and toward partner organizations. Pritchard suggested that NUL might need to catch up with peers with regard to providing new online services and scholarly communication-related programs and activities. The new UL wanted to raise Northwestern's profile in the research library community by increasing participation in cooperative initiatives and emphasizing the development of special collections, rare materials, and primary research resources.

Strategic Planning

Acknowledging the attractiveness—and also the potential expense—of the new UL's vision, the provost asked that Pritchard formulate a new strategic plan approximately one year after her arrival at Northwestern. The strategic plan would be the key to securing the university administration's support in turning Pritchard's ideals into reality. Library staff, students and faculty, library donors, and other stakeholders contributed ideas for the plan during the autumn of 2006 and the winter of 2007.

The first major decision was reached with the articulation of five goal areas and five strategies that would provide a framework for presenting more detailed objectives and proposed actions. The goal areas were 1) to advance student learning, 2) to support faculty research and teaching, 3) to sustain world class resources of long-term cultural importance, 4) to support the university's goals of interdisciplinarity and globalization, and 5) to ensure library readiness to meet campus needs. The strategies were 1) to improve digital infrastructure; 2) to increase collaboration and consortial participation with library, university, and other partners; 3) to develop services tailored to different user populations; 4) to transform physical spaces to enhance services and operational efficiency; and 5) to renew emphasis on unique collection strengths. Although these goals and strategies are not surprising or even unusual among ARL libraries, they do signal changes in organizational priority that are important to articulate. They also represent a significant expansion of the library's ambitions.

The second major decision resulted from an analysis of the suggestions and comments library staff and other stakeholders contributed in the initial stages of strategic planning. Few actually suggested reorganization, but many mentioned obstacles and limitations that seemed to be connected with the current administrative structure. Early in 2007 the UL suggested that adjustment to this structure would position NUL better for the future and would show the library's commitment to priorities for which it would soon seek funding. With the nervous support of the assistant university librarians, the UL announced to the library staff that the senior administrative team would be working on a new organization chart.

The Decision to Reorganize

At that time—and for many years before that—there were four major divisions in the NUL organization: the Public Services Division, the Technical Services Division, the Collection Management Division, and the Information Technology Division. Each division was led by an assistant university librarian. Each division was made up of departments defined by function, collection, or service location. Outside the division structure were several administrative units and individuals. Figure 6.1 (p. 68) shows this "before" situation.

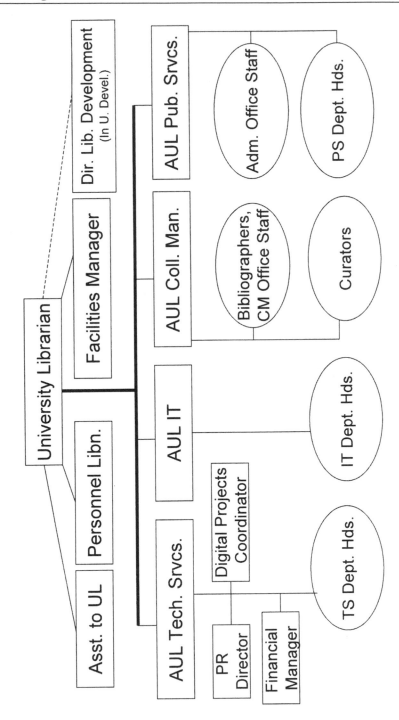

Figure 6.1. Northwestern University Library Reporting Lines of Senior Administrators before FY08 Reorganization.

Two features of the pre-FY 2008 organization are especially important to understand as part of the context for changes in the technical services part of the library. First, the library's financial manager, the director of public relations, and the coordinator of digital projects reported to the administrator with the title of AUL for technical services (AULTS), but they were not part of the Technical Services Division. Second, the AUL for collection management (AULCM) was responsible for a very wide range of functions, including planning, allocation, and management of the materials budget; collection analysis and evaluation; collections-related donor relations; and support for the work of approximately thirty selectors. The university archivist, the heads of several distinct libraries known as "curated collections," and several full-time bibliographers reported directly to the AULCM.

Echoing the comments of stakeholders, discussion in the senior management team focused on several challenges for the future and the corresponding weaknesses of the current organizational scheme:

- Responsibility for managing digital projects and digital collection building needed a more centralized organizational home. Units throughout the library organization needed to contribute significantly to digital library development. The pre-FY 2008 structure, relying on a part-time digital projects coordinator to recruit staff resources from diverse sources on a case-by-case basis, would not "scale" as the library's series of projects evolved into an ongoing, high-priority digital resources production program.

- The library's technology support operations needed more flexibility than seemed possible with the current departmental dividers. A more fluid, project team-based approach would be needed to meet a range of upcoming challenges. A recent problem accentuated the idea that a different organizational structure was needed: for several years the library had found it difficult to recruit and retain information technology professionals interested in traditional management and supervisory responsibilities.

- Operations connected with the management of purchased, licensed, and freely accessible electronic resources would require better automated systems and more staff resources in the future. It was becoming more and more difficult to draw lines between e-resource support functions according to technical services, public services, and information technology definitions. It was also becoming more and more difficult to "find someone" to do each new task or solve each new problem or support each new electronic resource.

- The complex and varied roles and responsibilities of the AULCM were becoming more difficult to address by a single administrator. This difficulty would surely be exacerbated, the team predicted, as the library increased its emphasis on developing and promoting special collections. It would be difficult for the AULCM to give special collections increased leadership attention while also managing the continuing transition of general collections to a more electronic form, planning for major collection shifts (e.g., to remote storage), and representing the library in negotiation and planning for consortial and cooperative purchasing deals.

- A more robust and responsive framework of subject specialist support for students and faculty was needed as part of a more coherent user services program. The new UL perceived the need to realign services in terms of academic programs and departments and to customize services for different kinds of users. Users could not be expected to understand, care about, or work around a cultural divide between bibliographers and reference librarians, collection management units and public services units; that divide had be erased.

Once these issues were articulated, possibilities for improvement were considered—usually in terms of adding new units to, or otherwise modifying, the existing divisions. No one equated the shuffling of names on an organizational chart with the achievement of goals to improve facilities, collections, and services. However, the senior administrative team did come to believe that reorganization could be an important step toward those improvements. A picture of positive change started to appear to the team when they focused on two of the issues discussed above: the need to provide a stronger administrative structure for digital library development and the need to facilitate a more coordinated approach to supporting academic units and programs. When decisions about those two issues were reached, other pieces of the organizational puzzle more easily fit into place.

The New Administrative Structure

Particularly difficult was the discussion about where in the organization a more centralized digital library unit should be placed. The senior administrative team finally decided that a new department should be partnered with others responsible for curating distinctive collections and rare materials in a new Special Libraries Division. This division would be led by the former AULCM. Existing digital production operations administered by preservation and multimedia services units would move into the new Digital Collections Department, as would responsibility for digital project management. In keeping with its placement in the organization, the new department would be focused on the development of distinctive digital resources, most produced locally or in cooperative projects. Information technology infrastructure and metadata support services would be provided by other units in other divisions. Most commercially produced electronic resources would be considered part of the general collections and would be managed elsewhere.

To strengthen service to academic units, the administrative team proposed the formation of an Academic Liaison Services Department. Two experienced bibliographers, formerly part of the Collection Management Division, would become subject specialists. Joining them would be one librarian transferred from the Reference Department, two subject specialists recruited from the outside, and the library's new scholarly communications librarian. In addition to supervising these librarians, the head of the Academic Liaison Services Department would organize and support a network of part-time subject specialists from throughout the library organization. The new department would be part of the Public Services Division, working with the Reference Department and other units to provide a suite of research consultation, instruction, curriculum support, and collection development services that would appear seamless to users but that could also be customized for different user groups.

But what would become of the remaining responsibilities traditionally carried out by the Collection Management Division? The senior administrative team suggested that responsibility for materials budget management, collection analysis, and other central collection development functions could be assigned to the current AULTS. She already supervised units responsible for the related functions of materials acquisitions and general financial operations. Clustering collection management support with these functions in a new division might facilitate integration of selection, acquisitions, and materials processing functions. It might also encourage the integration of collections budgeting with other financial operations. The group of departments resulting from the combination of central technical services (acquisitions, cataloging, serials control, and preservation), collection development support, and general business operations would be called the Technical Services and Resource Management (TS&RM) Division.

The senior administrative team further suggested that electronic resources management and collection development support services be combined in a single department within the new TS&RM division. This idea was inspired in part by the particular talents of the head of the Serials Department, who was experienced in both areas. His career exemplified the interconnection of electronic resources management issues with general collection management issues. In his role as acquisitions coordinator, he already worked closely with a collection analysis specialist who would be joining TS&RM. This positive collaboration inspired visions of a wonderful new team that could provide data-based decision and assessment support services useful to the entire library organization.

Late in the spring of 2007 the senior administrative team shared with library staff a proposed organizational structure based on these important ideas. Figure 6.2 (p. 72) shows the basics of the plan. In addition to establishing the three new departments mentioned above, the plan formalized a new arrangement for administrative functions—with the PR director reporting directly to the UL, and with a new director of administrative services assuming supervisory responsibility for facilities, personnel, and administrative office staff.

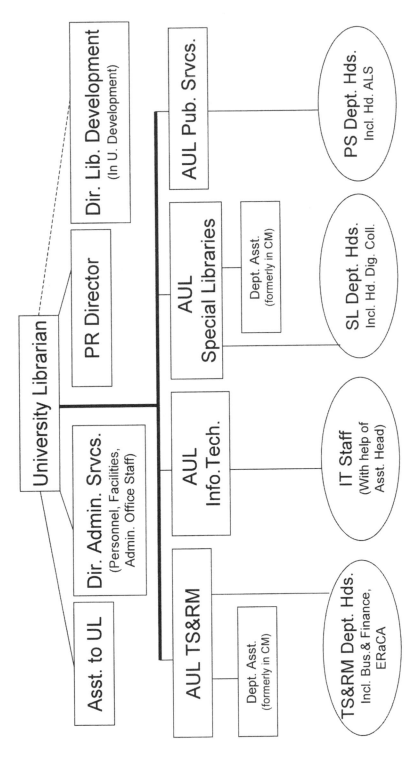

Figure 6.2. Northwestern University Library Reporting Lines of Senior Administrators after FY08 Reorganization.

It should be noted that, in addition to an administrative hierarchy, the new organization would feature five important interdivisional committees: a collections allocation committee, a digital projects committee, an instruction and outreach committee, a scholarly communication committee, and a Web services committee. These committees would have decision-recommending responsibilities that crossed divisional and department boundaries. A member of the senior administrative team would help facilitate the work of each committee. In addition, several coordinator positions would be defined. These individuals, usually not line supervisors, would be charged with organizing and supporting activities taking place in multiple administrative units. For instance, the coordinator of collections analysis would collect, organize, and report information that could be used for a variety of purposes all over the library organization.

Discussion of the reorganization plan outlined by the senior administrative team revealed that department heads were somewhat anxious about the potential makeup and authority of the four interdivisional teams. Everyone involved was a bit nervous about the distribution of formerly centralized collection management responsibility among three new divisions. The idea that permanent separate departments in the Information Technology Division might be replaced by project-based teams was mysterious to library staff, who wondered about implications for personnel classification and evaluation. On the whole, however, staff reaction was supportive of the concepts embedded in the proposed structure.

Staff comments inspired some refinements and adjustments, and the UL decided to move forward with the plan. One of those refinements was the decision to have the head of the new Academic Liaison Services Department report "with a dotted line" to the AULTS&RM for collection management-related issues. With the top level restructuring decisions outlined, each of the AULs was charged with developing a plan for organizing his or her new division and for contributing to the achievement of objectives within the library's new strategic goal areas.

The remainder of this chapter focuses on the organization of the new Technical Services and Resource Management Division.

Technical Services Challenges—New and Not-So-New

At the time this charge was issued, the Technical Services Division was made up of four departments: the Monographic Acquisitions and Rapid Cataloging (MARC) Department, the Catalog Department, the Serials Department, and the Preservation Department. As shown in Figure 6.3 (p. 74), each of these departments had a number of related responsibilities and a good sized staff. The AUL and four strong department heads formed a management team, working closely together to make sure that the division provided efficient and effective technical services for the general collections and most of the curated collections.

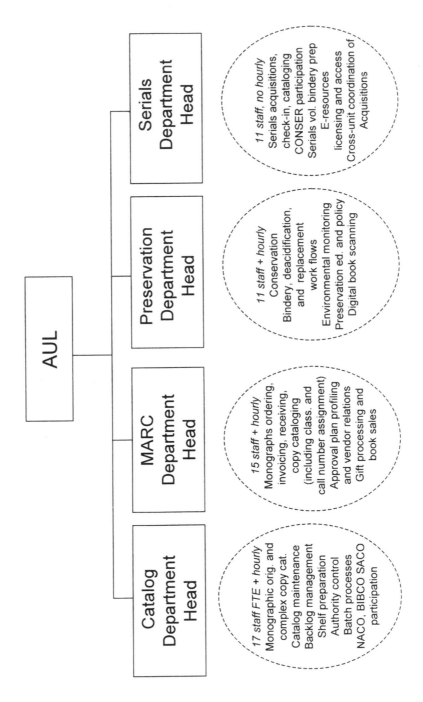

Figure 6.3. Technical Services Division Departments and Functions before FY08 Reorganization.

In the mid-1990s central technical services had been reorganized to take advantage of emerging vendor services such as electronic invoicing, and to maximize the effectiveness of the then-new Voyager library management system. The MARC, Catalog, and Serials Departments were formed at that time. This reorganization process had been highly successful, in that it provided a framework for implementing new work processes as a shared focus, rather than as an interruption of the "real work" or something one or more existing departments had to "add on." Effective interdepartmental workflows had been devised, particularly for the acquisition and processing of monographic material. Several backlogs were reduced or eliminated in the years following.

The Preservation Department was moved from the Collection Management Division to the Technical Services Division a few years after the other three departments were established. This change was made partly in recognition of the potential for streamlining the overall materials processing workflow through closer alignment of binding and conservation operations with acquisitions and cataloging. By 2006, however, it didn't seem that the potential for synergetic improvement based on that realignment had been realized. The AUL hoped to use the creation of the TS&RM Division to encourage more change.

Another not-so new challenge on the AUL's mind was management of electronic resources. Thus far, a few very busy people in the Serials Department had performed most licensing and other e-journal management tasks. Although not every electronic resource was strictly a serial, attempts to separate electronic acquisitions and cataloging work into monographic and serial varieties had not been very successful. The transition from paper journals to electronic journals was resulting in a decreasing workload for some staff; however, it was proving difficult to redeploy the time of those particular staff members directly to e-resource management work. A different strategy for matching available staff resources with priorities was needed.

In addition to tasks directly related to the acquisition of e-journals, some SFX- and MetaLib-related duties initially performed by staff in IT or public services departments were migrating to the Serials Department. The migrations made sense, but they blurred the line between direct service and backroom operations and strengthened the perception that the library needed a robust crew of staff specializing in electronic resources support work. To continue coping as the electronic collections grew, the library would need to choose and implement an electronic resources management system soon—or perhaps this change was already overdue. Even with the help of such a system, it seemed likely that staff time devoted to all aspects of electronic resources management would need to grow in the future; much of that work would be the responsibility of the TS&RM Division.

Selected NUL librarians had for some years been experimenting with metadata schemes and contributing to digital library projects by providing MARC and non-MARC metadata. Up to that time, staff hours devoted to metadata work for digital projects had been negotiated on a case-by-case basis.

This approach, characterized by full-time catalogers squeezing in time for metadata work on an occasional basis, would not scale appropriately to meet future demand for metadata services. The TS&RM Division would need to significantly expand its capacity to provide metadata support for digital projects. Such support would be needed for an increased number of projects organized by the new Digital Collections Department, but it would be needed also for projects initiated outside the library. The UL was interested in offering metadata consulting and/or production services to help NU faculty produce digital scholarship. This would be a new challenge for NUL, responsibility for which would fall to the TS&RM division.

The new TS&RM Division's mission would be significantly broader than that of the old Technical Services Division. Of particular concern was the acceptance of collection analysis and other collection development support responsibilities. Initially, some existing operations would need to be transferred from other divisions. A librarian and a full-time library assistant from the Collection Management Division would need new administrative homes somewhere in TS&RM. Fulfilling the new division's collection management responsibility would also require substantial amounts of time from the AUL—especially in the first year or two as she dealt with a significant learning curve. Later it would be necessary to analyze, expand, and improve services in the context of the new organization as well as a changing publishing environment and the library's expanded collection-building ambitions. In keeping with the UL's interest in increasing assessment activities throughout the library, the TS&RM Division would need to enhance its capabilities in data mining and analysis to support a broad range of resource allocation and service decisions.

The library would have to seriously consider vendor-provided technical services in connection with initiatives to enhance special collections and meet the needs of new university programs. The University Library would have to develop collections in East Asian languages, for instance, and build a new library to serve teaching programs planned for a Persian Gulf location. Also looming on the horizon was the strong possibility that the TS&RM Division would be asked to provide technical services for one or more non-NUL libraries in the near future. Potential cooperative initiatives involving the law and medical schools, a nearby seminary library, and the Northwestern University Press might involve trading services, sharing staff, or developing cross-unit work teams. Implementing nontraditional service operations would require planning, management, and coordination with existing local production operations.

Last but not least, increased emphasis on special collections would require a certain shift in focus for the central technical services units. For at least the previous two decades, technical services managers had been most interested in streamlining, standardization, taking advantage of cooperative opportunities, and automation. The technical services staff seemed relatively lean, and it focused considerable attention on production goals and backlog elimination/prevention. Uncovering hidden collections, developing new collections of rare or unique materials, and even creating new digital scholarly resources would require work that, by current standards, would be inefficient. Rather than such activities being done on an occasional basis, they would be part of the new division's "bread and butter." In the next few years, more positive management attention would have to be paid to fostering values of experimentation, operational research, and customizing records and procedures for special needs.

The New Division

As the internal structure of the new TS&RM Division was being planned in the summer of 2007, few of the challenges mentioned above were pressing urgently anywhere except in the mind of the AUL. It would have been possible to leave all the existing technical services departments intact, adding new assignments to each and making individual staffing shifts to meet specific needs in the future. Though easier in the short run, the AUL felt that such an approach would be unsound. Adding new assignments to the staff who seemed "closest" to each new challenge might result in units that were severely lopsided in level of staff development opportunity or administrative pressure. She liked the idea of rebalancing the burden of change, and the library's reorganization presented a good opportunity to do that. The AUL wanted to encourage managers and staff to embrace and devise strategies to fulfill the total mission of the new division, rather than to begrudge the library's new strategic agenda as a set of additional burdens falling on a few lucky or unlucky people.

In addition, the AUL wanted to show that TS&RM managers understood and were preparing to meet the technical services challenges inherent in the NUL strategic plan. It seemed important to make a statement to staff inside and outside the division that, although much of the library's new strategic plan focused on public service improvements, the plan's impact on technical services would be profound. The library organization did not have the capacity to support the improvements envisioned; increasing that capacity would require a strong, expandable technical services infrastructure. It was unlikely that the library would receive new resources sufficient to add significantly to technical services staffing, however. The TS&RM division would have to shift priorities and resources to support strategic initiatives. Technical services business could not just go on in the future as it had in the past. That message might be reinforced by changes in the organization of technical services staff and activities.

All the steps in reorganization—developing new unit names and new lists of responsibilities, analyzing the staffing needs for each, making changes in reporting lines and assignments, training and learning tasks formerly performed by others—could help prepare the division to meet the challenges ahead. It had happened that way a decade earlier with the Voyager-related reorganization. The AUL decided to risk short-term discontent among staff who might feel themselves organizationally displaced for "no good reason" and push for organizational changes that anticipated the future as well as facilitating current initiatives. She encouraged managers and staff to look for opportunities for change suggested, though not necessarily required immediately, by the library's reorganization.

The TS&RM management team started meeting regularly a couple of months prior to the proposed "reorganization day." The managers quickly articulated three assumptions on which to continue planning. First, there would be five departments in the new TS&RM Division. The heads of the four existing technical services units and the head of business and finance were all available; there was no reason not to take advantage of the talents of all five. Second, the business and finance staff of just five full-time employees would initially be moved into the TS&RM Division as a unit. At least for the short term, it seemed prudent to maintain a distinct financial operations staff. Third, the rest of the staff in the former Technical Services Division would be arranged into four departments, each of which would face a mixture of continuing responsibilities and new challenges.

The next step was to work out how the responsibilities and challenges could best be divided and translated into coherent department missions. The management team devised a basic plan, discussed the ideas in it with staff who would potentially be affected most or soonest, and then presented the plan at a meeting combining staff of both the "old" Technical Services Division and the "new" TS&RM Division. Refinements in the plan continued as staff and managers talked through specific issues. Staff members who were apprehensive about getting new supervisors were given special attention, meeting with potential new colleagues and beginning any necessary training well before reorganization day.

At that point the unit names were not settled, and some of the departments had difficulty deciding on what names would best convey their missions. Figure 6.4 shows the names that were later decided on: Acquisitions and Rapid Cataloging (ARC), Bibliographic Services, Business and Finance, Electronic Resources and Collection Analysis (ERaCA), and Preservation.

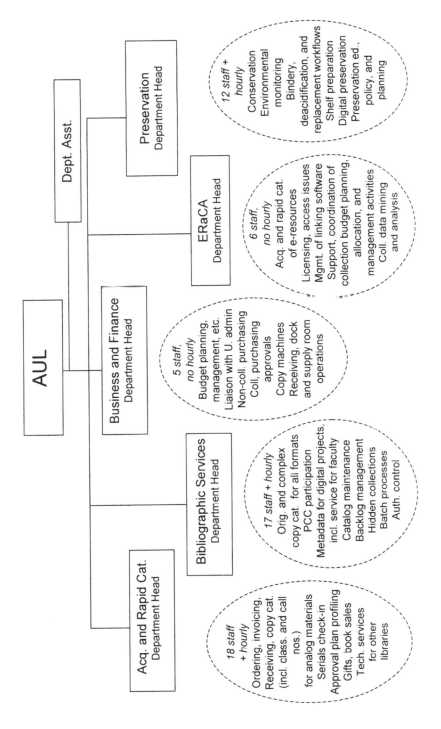

Figure 6.4. Technical Services and Resource Management Division Departments and Functions after FY08 Reorganization.

Whither Serials?

The most difficult and controversial challenge in defining the departments of TS&RM concerned the placement of serials acquisitions, check-in, and cataloging duties. As part of the previous reorganization, all serials functions had been put together in one department. This arrangement had been reasonably successful for almost a decade, and it was difficult for some staff members to envision any other way of getting serials work done. Many electronic resources are serial in nature, and the head of ERaCA is a serials expert. Therefore, they argued, the ERaCA Department should have responsibility for all serials management functions in addition to electronic resources and collection analysis work. Such an arrangement would be easier for the staff than the alternatives discussed, and it would result in departments that were more balanced in terms of staff size.

Acknowledging the validity of that logic, the AUL nevertheless pressed the unit managers for a different solution. She was interested in a new approach to serials acquisitions and cataloging that would serve the library appropriately during a period in which the number of paper serials would continue to decrease, particularly in the general collections. She hoped that the process of integrating serials and monographs workflows as much as possible might result in improved turnaround time for print serials processing, more flexible staffing possibilities, and increased reliance on vendor services and automation. She wanted to get some fresh eyes looking at the mainstream workflows for both serials and monographs, with a goal of reducing staff resources for both. She also wanted to free the head of the new ERaCA department to concentrate on the electronic resources management and collection analysis challenges that would be so strategically important in the next few years.

The managers responded to the AUL's challenge, ultimately settling on a plan to distribute the staff and duties formerly located in the Serials Department among four departments of the new TS&RM Division. The ERaCA Department would be responsible for acquisitions, licensing, catalog record identification, and rapid copy cataloging for electronic journals and databases. The head of the Serials Department and three other individuals already engaged in e-resources work would join ERaCA. The staff of the former serials acquisitions section would join the ARC Department. ARC staff would acquire, check in, and identify copy, and catalog most nonelectronic journals. They would work together with colleagues from ERaCA in situations, now diminishing in frequency, when the library wanted to receive both paper and electronic versions. Staff of the serials cataloging section would join the Bibliographic Services Department, which would be responsible for cataloging serials requiring original or complex copy cataloging. Catalog management staff in Bibliographic Services would begin processing serial withdrawals and transfers. Staff in the Preservation Department would assume responsibility for serials volume work connected directly with binding.

The New Departments

Thus, where once there was a MARC Department, there is now a slightly larger ARC Department. Not limiting its scope of responsibility to processing monographs, the new ARC Department will experiment with integrating serials and monographic work flows. The ARC management team has also been challenged to reengineer and/or reduce serials check-in and claiming activities. ARC will coordinate and manage the vendor-supplied technical services that should play an important role in NUL's ability to meet new collection development challenges over the next few years. The ARC Department, more than any of the other departments, retains an emphasis on speedy, streamlined production processes and tries to minimize item-by-item decision making in favor of automated and vendor-assisted processes and routines.

On the other hand, the Bibliographic Services Department specializes in work that is more difficult to streamline. The department still must be interested in efficiency, and devising automated processes to improve efficiency is part of its mission. The Bibliographic Services Department's overall role, however, is to invent solutions to problems, take care of nonroutine challenges, and help develop special collections. The majority of librarians in the TS&RM division have their administrative homes in Bibliographic Services. Original cataloging, authority control, and catalog maintenance functions are concentrated there. Bibliographic Services personnel coordinate the cataloging work of multiple units contributing to a shared library management system database and to the Program for Cooperative Cataloging. A metadata unit within Bibliographic Services will work hand-in-glove with the new Digital Collections Department, providing metadata support for digital projects, growing a metadata consulting service for faculty, and coordinating metadata standards and procedures for the library's emerging digital repository.

As noted previously, the name, staff configuration, and basic mission of the Business and Finance Department remains unchanged for now. Serving the entire library and providing the library's communication link with campus administrative units, the Business and Finance staff can facilitate changes related to the library's reorganization and strategic plan. The entire library will come through the current reorganization better, if the business office and receiving room can function as constant, dependable resources for everyone. In the meantime, the Business and Finance Department head is also leading the library's implementation of Northwestern's new automated financial systems.

For an initial period of a year or so, the staff of Business and Finance will get used to being part of a division and look for ideas for future collaboration, cross training, and adjustments in staffing patterns and assignments. Having worked with this unit closely for several years before the reorganization, the AUL is confident that such opportunities will be found and that good things will come of the inclusion of Business and Finance in the TS&RM Division. At the very first meeting of TS&RM department heads, for instance, an adjustment to the workflow involving credit card purchase of library materials emerged from the conversation.

The new Electronic Resources and Collection Analysis (ERaCA) Department is being set up as the center of collection management support and electronic resources management activities. These two functions may become less distinct and more integrated as more resources are devoted to electronic collection development. The ERaCA Department staff is relatively small now, comprising one librarian and two library assistants concentrating on electronic resources work, a librarian whose primary assignment is collection analysis, the head, and a library assistant who helps with everything. Another staff member coming to the TS&RM Division through reorganization reports directly to the AUL. This department assistant supports the AUL in her new work as collection development officer, but she also works very closely with ERaCA staff on collection analysis and other collection management support work.

The Preservation Department didn't get a new name, but underwent two significant changes as part of the reorganization. Staff engaged in digital reformatting using a robotic page-turning book scanner moved Preservation to the new Digital Collections Department in the Special Libraries Division. The head of the Preservation Department, however, retains responsibility for leadership in the establishment of digital preservation standards, policies, and procedures as part of digital repository development. The library's shelf preparation unit, until recently part of the Catalog Department, joined the Preservation Department. The library reorganization provided a good opportunity to implement this adjustment, which had been informally discussed as a possibility several times before. Initial benefits of this change came quickly: during get-acquainted meetings, shelf preparation staff and their soon-to-be colleagues in the Preservation Department identified several streamlining or resource-saving measures they could implement immediately.

Location, Location, Location . . .

One of NUL's most difficult current problems is insufficient space. Money for a major library space planning study has already been budgeted by the university. The study will take place in the next year or so. In addition to proposing the transfer of some collections to remote storage and the revitalization of public spaces in library facilities, the study will help plan and configure staff spaces appropriate to the organizational structure. There is a shared hope among the library staff that their work areas will be improved within the next few years.

In the meantime, staff must more or less stay where they are. Current library spaces are not flexible enough to permit much change, and it would seem foolhardy to invest significant resources in renovation prior to the completion of the space study. With the exception of a few workstation swaps that might be negotiated on a case-by-case basis, no physical changes are occurring as part of the FY 2008 library reorganization. In some cases this means that unit heads are separated from some of the staff they supervise, and work units are dispersed among several areas.

Implementing a new administrative structure without being able to move staff workstations wouldn't have been the library administration's first choice, but this constraint has a bright side. The limitations of the current space did not define the limits of possible change in organizational structure. Furthermore, the knowledge that "no one is moving any time soon" lowered staff anxiety and encouraged creativity in thinking about organizational change. Staff could consider possibilities for changes in administrative structure without the distraction of worries over potential improvement or degradation of their physical work environment. It is also easing the transition for longtime colleagues who have been split up administratively as part of reorganization. Those colleagues are still as physically handy to each other as they ever were.

Anticipating Success

The reporting line changes required by the plan described above took place in the fall of 2007. An initial focus of staff in the new units is necessarily to make sure routine processes and services continue and that nothing has "fallen through the cracks" of the new organization. Mission statements, job descriptions, and Web pages will be adjusted to reflect the new organization over the next few months. It is likely that staff with new organizational perspectives will start to envision adjustments in ongoing workflows and procedures. It will be important to capture all the ideas that result from learning new duties and building fresh relationships, even if those ideas cannot all be implemented, or even seriously considered, immediately. Of particular importance will be to follow up on "Why do we even do that?" and "Why is that important?" questions. Such questions may uncover opportunities to shift priorities and make room for new kinds of work.

Each of the TS&RM departments is devising its own internal structure, and each has been encouraged to create units, teams, and supervisory relationships that look forward several years. Although departments can reorganize themselves any time, the formation of the new division provides an opportunity to be bold in good company. The Bibliographic Services Department, for instance, will likely name an assistant department head and a manager to organize a future metadata consulting service. The Preservation Department may define an organizational place to grow its capacity for rare books conservation. ARC may define a team to encourage faster integration of serials and monographs processing. ERaCA will probably set up a structure that anticipates some staff growth and the future use of an electronic resources management system. The

Business and Finance Department will probably take a more evolutionary approach, but joining the TS&RM Division should give the department a more supportive environment for defining opportunities, analyzing problems, and planning changes than it has ever had before.

In the meantime, the division as a whole and each department will be asked to articulate some goals related to the library's strategic priorities. Those goals will have to be supported by plans for achieving them. The goals will define the contributions the division can make to the library's success in the next few years, and the proof of the reorganization pudding will be in the plans. Experience suggests that groups of people in organizations can surpass the expectations of their leaders in both productivity and creativity if they are provided with a supportive, yet challenging, environment. It is hoped that Northwestern University Library's reorganization will help create such an environment for technical services. The reorganization will succeed if it helps the AUL, managers, and staff of the new TS&RM Division to develop plans that disregard former organizational boundaries and use all available resources to meet challenges that face the library now and in the future.

7

Sizes of Change: Improving Technical Services Efficiency at a Regional Public Library

Daniel Sifton

Like their colleagues in public services, technical services employees must continually adapt and evolve to keep pace with changes—often driven by technology—that push at the library from all directions. The most visible changes are naturally those demanded by patrons, but the changes to the "back end" may often have the greatest impact.

The Cariboo Regional District Library (CRDL) is a midsized public library system consisting of fifteen branches covering a rural landscape roughly the same size as the state of Indiana. The headquarters and main branch share office space with the local government, the Cariboo Regional District, and are located in Williams Lake, British Columbia. Relatively isolated from the engine of the province, Williams Lake is a seven-hour drive northeast from Vancouver. With a service population area of 70,000, this region is one of the most sparsely populated in the province. All communities, however, regardless of their size, deserve the best that a library has to offer, especially those with limited access to information simply because of their location. To give an indication of the level of isolation, it is worth noting that at the time of this writing, a handful of the branches were still without high-speed Internet access (the story of Internet connectivity at the Cariboo Regional District Library is another story altogether).

The Technical Services Department at this library is much like that at others, albeit on a smaller scale; workflows are regularly assessed, cataloging output is monitored, and technological challenges occur frequently.

Structure and Function

The department currently consists of 4.12 full-time employees (FTEs). Working relationships at CRDL are close and with limited overlap, in a small workspace. From the library's inception in 1994, cataloging has been performed by library technicians, of whom there are currently two FTEs. There is a single full-time acquisitions clerk, a .60 FTE processing clerk, and recently an ILL clerk at .60 FTE has been added.

Reduced cataloging output led to the recent creation of an interlibrary loan (ILL) clerk position. Prior to this, ILL duties were shared by the cataloging staff on a rotating basis. One cataloger would perform ILL duties in the afternoon, while the other would catalog new and added items. Each month they would trade duties, in an effort to build some redundancy into the system. Under this formula, followed for years, slowdowns in cataloging productivity were routinely addressed by reducing the time allotted to ILL duties, in smaller and smaller increments. This approach, while satisfying immediate cataloging requirements, was clearly unworkable in the long term. Confined to the afternoon in order to limit their extent—it was believed that if ILL duties were undertaken in the morning they could potentially consume the greater part of the day—ILL duties began to creep backward to meet the increasing demand, further reducing cataloging output.

On average, cataloging output was 1,100–1,300 pieces per month, and significantly less when a cataloger was absent (600–800). With only 1.5 FTE catalogers (ILL was .5), an absence would reduce the number not by half, but by two-thirds, as ILL duties would still be assigned for the required half day and cataloging for the remaining half (see figure 7.1).

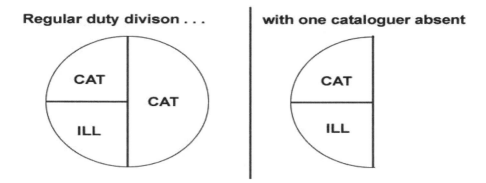

Regular duty divison . . .

with one cataloguer absent

Figure 7.1. CRDL Technical Services Staffing.

It can be seen that with a large number of planned and unplanned absences in the form of conferences, illnesses, and vacations, additions would slow to a trickle (it is worth noting that between them the cataloging staff members have over fifty available annual vacation days). In 2004 the department saw three bereavement leaves in a three-month period, bracketed on both sides by conferences and vacations. The already shaky system soon began to show signs of breaking.

Trouble in the Wilderness

In the fall of that same year, branches began with increasing frequency to note the limited volume of materials being received. Statistical reports confirmed the slowdown, but did not provide any solutions.

Staff and management met repeatedly during the early days of the crisis in an effort to identify the roots of the problem and apply a solution. Soliciting input from staff on organizational and traditionally "managerial" topics has improved morale in the department, creating a safe environment in which staff members are increasingly comfortable expressing their views and proposing new ideas. Many of the improvements explored here have their origins in staff suggestions, not those of management. Although difficult to quantify, the resulting improvement to morale has undoubtedly had an effect on workplace efficiency.

Months before output had begun to slow down, a decade's worth of statistical data had been converted to a digital format. Prior to this initiative, all statistics had been recorded on paper. The digitized data revealed some key trends that proved critical to solving the crisis. Chief among these was the marked decline in cataloging output, the steady rise of the materials budget (with more funds, there are more items to catalog), and a doubling of interlibrary loan traffic over a five-year period. As noted, previous attempts to increase additions by limiting ILL duties had been unsuccessful. Until now, no one had considered the problem of trying to shoe-horn twice the workload into a reduced time frame.

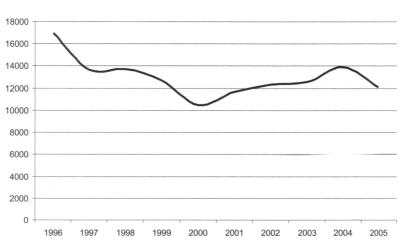

Figure 7.2. Cataloging Additions, 1996–2005.

The high point in figure 7.2, 17,000 pieces reported for 1996, occurred with the addition of a third cataloguer. From 1997 onward the cataloging department was composed of two catalogers working the discussed CAT/ILL split .

The budget, although dynamic, has experienced an overall increase over the same time period (see figure 7.3). With few exceptions, cataloging output has followed a similar path to that of the materials budget. In 2000 the library lent 722 items. Five years later that number stood at 1,570. (See figure 7.4.) Although lending has doubled, it is worth noting that borrowing traffic has also significantly increased.

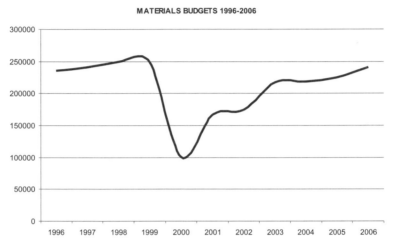

Figure 7.3. Materials Budgets, 1996–2006.

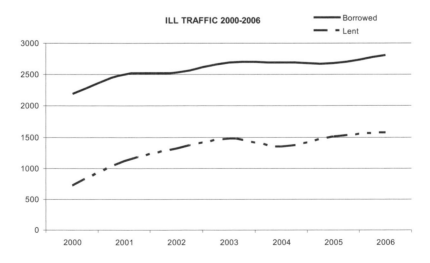

Figure 7.4. ILL Traffic, 2000–2006.

Multiple Answers

It must be noted that the statistics were not the only evidence of productivity problems; one need only observe and converse with staff members for that. The statistics became evidence for the justification of a new position, one that, due to budget limitations, was still over a year away. In the meantime, many smaller measures were discussed and implemented, in the hopes that collectively they would alleviate some of the problems. Even without the addition of a new staff member, these temporary solutions proved to be remarkably effective, and included the following:

- **Scanner reconfiguration:** Traditionally technical services staff searched for titles—either in receiving or in cataloging—via title or author keyword browsing. Bar code scanners at each station were configured to allow for ISBN scanning, allowing for a much quicker search process.

- **Reduced processing:** Following a growing trend at many libraries, the pocket label that had been printed and placed in the inside cover was eliminated. As it is the catalogers who print and place labels, fewer labels meant less time labeling and more time cataloging, as well as a reduction in label expenses.

- **New bibliographic utility:** The current ILS at CRDL prevents the use of Z39.50 inside the application. With the dissolution of LaserQuest, the library purchased BookWhere, a Web-based Z39.50 client, at a tenth of the cost. In addition, the new product allows for the retrieval of a substantial number of VHS/DVD records. LaserQuest was notably weak in this area.

- **Added copies:** In the past these copies were identified and added by cataloguing staff. The acquisitions clerk, previously limited to ordering and receiving new materials, now identifies and inserts added copies into the ILS upon receipt. Unlike cataloging, the library's Acquisition Department experiences considerable fluctuations throughout the year. Incorporating additional duties into this position was a simple process. Of all the quick fixes, this initiative has had the greatest impact on productivity and is perhaps the most far reaching. Branches identify which copies are duplicates and mark their orders accordingly before submitting them to acquisitions. And as every item passes through the clerk's hands, this individual also makes note of duplicates. The ordering records are marked in the ILS to allow for quick identification upon receipt. Some titles are bound to be missed, but last year added copies inserted into the database this way accounted for 11 percent of total cataloging output.

The department also applied and then retracted other solutions that were deemed ineffective:

- **Outsourcing:** A brief analysis revealed outsourcing to be of limited value even when confined to a specific format, such as DVDs. It was not the most cost-effective solution, nor would it contribute anything to staff morale.

- **Classification Web:** Technologically, the members of the department are late adapters. The CRDL experiment with Classification Web experienced many of the negative results of Ferris's study, wherein lack of training and technological aptitude hindered success (2006, 132).

The changes listed above eliminated much of the existing backlog and prevented a new one from developing. At the same time, they allowed the department to illustrate that numerous approaches were being pursued, while simultaneously lobbying for a budget increase and the creation of a new position dedicated to ILL processing. After adopting the solutions, cataloging additions increased by 30 percent in the following year, and as a result cataloging levels have surpassed the high point of 1996, when there were three full-time catalogers. Figure 7.5 shows the resultant spike in additions in the 2005–2006 year.

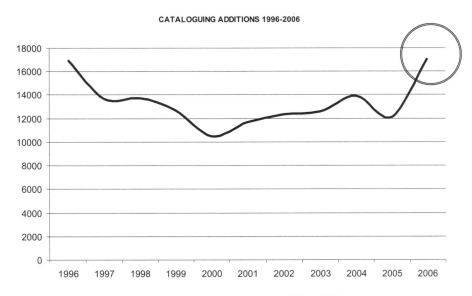

Figure 7.5. Cataloging Additions 1996–2006.

These successes did not eliminate the need for a new position. ILL traffic shows no sign of diminishing. In fact, early numbers for the 2007 year showed the increase continuing at the same rate. Nor would the library consider any attempts to decrease this service—as one of its provincial operating grants is directly linked to ILL volume. Moreover, with only two catalogers, the problems associated with absences, planned or otherwise, are likely to return. Increased specialization has substantially improved efficiency in the department. Since the ILL position has been created, however, successes in the cataloging department have led to difficulties in another.

Processing

As the number of additions significantly improved, the increased flow of materials created strains in processing. The processing clerk retired, and the learning curve associated with the new employee prompted the department to consider a new round of small "solutions." Among them was the assignment of spine labeling to catalogers and, more important, the assignment of bar code application to the acquisitions clerk. These changes are best illustrated by the examination of both past and present workflows in the Technical Services Department.

Workflows

In the past, processing at the library was a two-stage process. Upon arrival, new items would first be received and then placed in a queue for processing, only to be returned to processing a few days or weeks later. Figure 7.6 (p. 92) traces the original path.

Here, the new materials traveled from the receiving table (A) to the acquisitions clerk (B) and the preprocessing shelves (C), where they were removed by the processing clerk at (D) for security strips, jackets, stamps, pockets, and bar codes. After preprocessing, items were placed in the queue to be cataloged at (E). The catalogers (F) then created/copied records as required before returning the materials to the final processing shelves (G), where the clerk (H) applied covering labels and mack-tack, before shipping the materials to the branches (I).

Visualized, it was a confusing and convoluted knot that created a feedback loop (from B to E). That loop added to the general "noise" of the system by creating undue pressure on the processing clerk. In this scenario, the clerk would have to monitor two input streams—those items ready for preprocessing and those ready for final processing—continually assessing which was most important. With the acquisitions clerk now applying bar codes upon receipt, the remaining processing is transferred to the final (now single) stage of the processing circuit. This effort also resulted in some supply cost reductions, as a bar code cover was no longer necessary when the bar codes were applied prior to the book jackets.

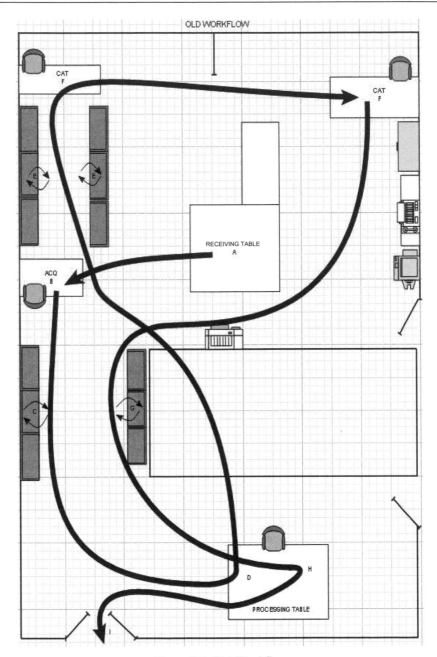

Figure 7.6. Old Workflow.

The revised path shown in figure 7.7 is straightforward even at a casual glance, illustrating the simplicity of a system in which the only pressure is the steady influx of materials and their movement from one end to another.[1] Here new items move from the receiving table (A) to the acquisitions clerk (B), who receives, attaches a bar code, and then adds them to the cataloging queue (C). After creating or copying records the catalogers (D) then bring the items forward to the processing shelves (E), where they are retrieved by the processing clerk (F) for security strips, jackets, and stamps before being shipped to the branches (G).

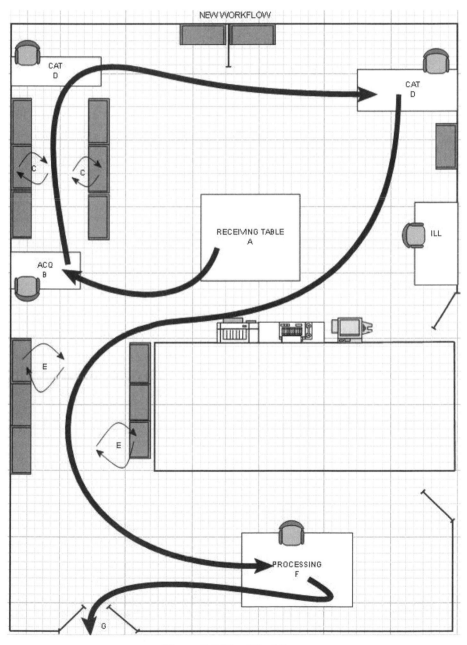

Figure 7.7. New Workflow.

The Future

As a cohesive whole, these improvements have now been in place since January 2007. In that time the department has seen two retirements and gained three new employees (including the ILL clerk) in processing and acquisitions. During this transition period, additions are still at optimum levels, averaging 1,500–1750 pieces per month. The system appears to be working, yet the future will likely contain new obstacles and necessitate new improvements. Currently under consideration are dual-monitor workstations for each of the catalogers; separate work and search screens should further increase efficiency. A proposed ILS migration (fall 2008) is likely to have a significant impact on cataloging additions, not to mention a possible redesign of optimum workflows.

With the retirements, some of the redundancy that was built into the system—a product of long-term staff retention—will need to return. In the past, staff members were always confident, if not comfortable, performing another's duties in an emergency. Such diversity will need to be included in future training. Finally, because the processing clerk is also responsible for ordering a growing number of supplies, the department, and the library as a whole, would benefit if this position were expanded to full time.

Conclusion

For years now, change has been a constant at the CRDL. It has come in various shapes and sizes and been driven by a variety of forces, but the changes initiated and met by staff have had the greatest impact on productivity and morale. In the department some functions have been concentrated in one individual, while others have been best improved by diversification. As a team, the department continually looks for improvements, constantly refining its efforts, striving to anticipate coming challenges. And if past successes are any indication, it is well prepared for the inevitable changes yet to come.

Endnote

1. Not all preprocessing can be avoided. Many audiovisual items must receive new cases (bar codes must be attached to the new case before cataloging) and security strips prior to being inserted in the cataloging queue. But because the bulk of the library's materials are not AV items, this path does not appear in the diagram.

References

Ferris, Anna M. 2006. If you buy it, will they use it?: A case study on the use of Classification Web. *Library Resources & Technical Services* 50 (2): 129–37. Available at EBSCOhost (accessed September 4, 2008).

8

Staffing Trends in Academic Library Technical Services: A Qualitative Analysis

Vicki Toy Smith

This chapter is a follow-up to a chapter in *Innovative Redesign and Reorganization of Library Technical Services* (Eden 2004), "Staffing Trends in Academic Technical Services" (Smith and Etcheverria 2004, 41–51). The effects of technological innovation on technical services administrators' experiences is the focus of this follow-up study. The present qualitative analysis provides more clarity on a reported general trend in academic library technical services units. The 2004 chapter on staffing trends examined the issue of changing roles for librarians in technical services departments. This follow-up analysis suggests that the roles of professional librarians in technical services units are in a state of unpredictable and constant change. Part of the ongoing change is due to the impact of electronic resources in libraries.

One hundred six questionnaires were mailed to managers in technical services units in academic libraries throughout the United States. Of those surveyed, twenty-five administrators entered valid responses. The survey results indicated that the number of years of service provide a "great deal of insight into the changing role technical services units are playing in academic libraries"(Smith and Etcheverria 2004, 47). Academic technical services units have had to embrace new technology, specifically electronic resources, while also coming to terms with diminishing staff as positions are "eliminated or reassigned to other departments"(Smith and Etcheverria 2004, 47). The dissatisfaction of professionals in technical services departments was difficult to ignore in the survey results. (See chapter appendix for the original survey, which took place in 2003.) The perception of increased work with a lack of corresponding growth in library roles and recognition among professionals, coupled with a large segment reporting dissatisfaction, points to a real problem: increased marginalization in technical services units. Upon closer examination of the surveys received, it was apparent that a "segment of the staff, those who trained paraprofessionals to take on increasing responsibility in cataloging and acquisitions processes, remains to be tapped for its wealth of experience and ability"(Smith and Etcheverria 2004, 47). Such findings can contribute to potential retooling of workflows and maximized overall job satisfaction for technical services librarians.

Technological Changes, Technical Services, and Experience

Despite a variety of technological changes in the profession and published statistical information on changing trends in technical services (Mitchell 2007; Eden 2004; Calhoun 2003), there is a deficit of qualitative information on the topic of role changes in technical services administration. In fact, few papers have been published that examine role changes from a managerial perspective in technical services units. This is confirmed by Norm Medeiros's article (2005) on influences on competency perceptions and expectations of technical service administrators, which asserts that "it may not be unreasonable to believe that less senior administrators are more familiar with these technologies" than higher level ones. A significant number of respondents in Medeiros's survey revealed that technology often left them less knowledgeable about how to deal with everyday activities. The research resulting from the Smith and Etcheverria survey can shed further light on technological challenges for today's technical services administrators. The majority of the survey respondents cited in the 2004 chapter stated that technology has a tremendous impact on the changes taking place in technical services units (Smith and Etcheverria 2004, 47). The issue of job satisfaction is crucial and needs closer examination.

Technology and new demands by patrons, who are faced with an ever-expanding universe of electronic journals and the influence of Google, have changed the way librarians deal with planning and new developments. Following is an examination of how this change is affecting the roles of administrators throughout technical services departments.

Selection Criteria

As a follow-up to the original survey, e-mails were sent to eight of the original group surveyed. These eight people had expressed interest in being contacted during the original survey. Five of those contacted responded. Of the five interviewees, three were women and two were men. Three of the survey respondents were heads of technical services, one was a director of collection management and resource acquisitions, and another was associate director of central technical services. These five administrators represent a cross-section of areas in technical services units. Although there are fewer men than women in libraries, this in-depth study included 40 percent male respondents.

In the follow-up qualitative survey, an attempt was made to develop a dialogue on topics that can spotlight various aspects of change occurring in technical services units. Topics covered included outsourcing, retirement of catalog/technical services librarians, moving professional activities to classified staff, the MARC record being marginalized, and views on faculty status among technical services librarians. A number of questions were asked:

What changes in the world of librarianship have had the greatest personal impact on your work as a technical services professional?

In what ways have you been impacted?

If you are in the library field five years from now, what do you see yourself doing?

How different will that be from work you do today?

What changes do you see for the future of library paraprofessionals?

How have staffing changes in your library influenced your work and your job performance?

Does the size of your library affect your level of job satisfaction?

Do librarians at your institution have faculty status? If so, is faculty status a factor in your level of job satisfaction?

Overall, when you think about broad changes in the library field that have impacted the nature of your work, do you view them in a negative or a positive light (or both)? Why?

Findings

Following are observations from the interviews done with the five participants. A number of major trends surfaced from the interviews:

- **Change noted by participants as having the greatest personal impact is technology.** All respondents commented on the fact that advances in technology were the single greatest factor that has affected work environments, job duties and descriptions, and their own personal job satisfaction. Some respondents discussed these changes in positive tones, some in negative tones, and some in both positive and negative tones. One administrator, who started his career thirty-five years ago, reflected on the impact of creating and implementing catalog records via OCLC, integrated systems, microform and online catalogs, and electronic resources (Bierman 2005). The rapid growth and continual changes in the world of electronic resources have continued to have a huge impact on the workflow. Although new jobs and positions have been created, an increased supervisory role has become the norm. Accurate job descriptions within a university's bureaucratic structure have become difficult to define (Lewis 2005). Although technology was supposed to make library tasks easier, the opposite has taken place. Although more records have appeared so that less original cataloging has to be done, "the complexity of the records, the various formats, the questions of how to handle, what to catalog, what to link—have increased dramatically"(Ramsay 2005). Another respondent stated that the "effort to keep up with the amount of information and the costs of making the materials available" have taxed administrators' skills.

- **Technology made life both simpler and more complex.** Life has become simpler because catalogers find more records in utilities (although likely a consequence of more contributions, not more sophisticated technology). One administrator stated that the mechanics of work has become much simpler (Nuzzo 2005), yet original cataloging has become more difficult. Training needs and users' needs have become even greater. The survey showed that respondents spent much more time with tools than with content (Mueller 2005). This was an interesting reaction within a field that is often more about tools than content, but the sense of it left the librarian frustrated. There have been pros and cons to all the technological changes. Issues can be resolved much more quickly given the electronic world, but on the negative side, things can also get lost and be irretrievable. So much information is available that it has become unwieldy and confusing for patrons, who have no conception of what is authoritative and what is not.

- **All mentioned staff reductions.** All of the respondents referred to the diminishing staff in their library. One respondent mentioned that staff in her technical services units had been reduced by 50 percent. Technical services administrators have had to come to grips with increasing cost effectiveness in their units. Another respondent mentioned that a growing number of retirements have had an additional impact. One administrator mentioned that new positions had been created in the department, but referred to the fact that "roles are changing"(Lewis 2005). All referred to the reality of more work for all department members. With a decrease in staff in technical services, more time has to be spent refining workflows and eliminating unnecessary steps. One librarian stated that although this has not necessarily been a problem, there comes a point at which the administrator has run out of possible solutions to solve workflow issues (Nuzzo 2005). Technical services administrators have had to depend on paraprofessionals a great deal more. There has been a growing need for additional training of staff. As things change, professionals have had to keep up with technological changes and then become teachers and trainers for their staff members (Lewis 2005).

- **Public services staff was perceived to increase, while technical services staff was decreasing.** Although there is a demand for librarians in the public services sector, it appears to many that technical services staff is diminishing. It has been suggested that when catalog librarians retire, replacements may not be hired. With the MARC record becoming marginalized, the demand for catalogers using the MARC record may very well decline. There has been talk of XML and other types of metadata structures impacting the MARC record. Terry Reese (2007) has reflected on the issue of traditional formats (MARC and AACR2) and RDA continuing to isolate the technical services community. There may be no way to predict a future in which higher administration has asked for an alternative to the traditional MARC record and the online catalog as it appears today. With faceted searching and other products offered by vendors such as Endeca, Medialab Solutions, and Innovative Interfaces, the technical services landscape will be changed even more. Several of the respondents indicated that there would be fewer professional MLS catalogers in the future. It has been clear that catalogers will be forced to become "database managers who manage the outsourcing contracts and manage the integration of the records they receive into the local catalog database " (Bierman 2005). Public services departments have had an increase in personnel since everything has become much more complex. More personnel are needed to educate the community (information literacy, ask a librarian online (chat), blogs, etc.) (Ramsay 2005).

- **Some respondents saw outsourcing as an impact on technical services as a profession**. There has been an increased need for more outsourcing. In the case of special types of cataloging, this outsourcing can be done by entrepreneurial catalogers who can provide outsourcing of cataloging, "especially in niche specialized markets (music scores, foreign languages, etc." (Bierman 2005). In addition, technical services departments will look to vendors (e.g., OCLC, Serials Solutions) to purchase various types of bibliographic records. There are forces already in place (increased effectiveness, the pending retirement of over half of the U.S. catalogers in the next five to ten years, etc.) that will require many libraries to outsource much of their cataloging—including, and perhaps especially, original cataloging. Entrepreneurial catalogers can set themselves up to provide contract cataloging services on a contractual/piece basis. (Bierman 2005).

- **Some participants saw their involvement with public services increasing.** At least one participant noted an increased involvement with public services. The respondent noted a clouding of lines between what was traditionally called public services (the umbrella heading for reference service, document delivery, reserves, and circulation) and traditional technical services, where cataloging and acquisitions take place. One respondent suggested that outreach endeavors to patrons would increase in the course of increased involvement.

- **Participants saw an increased/increasing role for paraprofessionals.**
  Most foresaw more responsibility for paraprofessional employees in technical services, increased engagement, and additional involvement in departmental concerns. One administrator mentioned the possibility of the blurring between the role of the professional and the role of the paraprofessional, as the latter takes on increased responsibility in supervision and decreased clerical work. One respondent surmised that low-level work will stop altogether as it is perceived to be increasingly low in priority, or that low-priority work would be outsourced.

- **Roles of professionals were also changing and becoming increasingly removed from day to day operations in technical services.** Roles of professionals were also seen to be expanding or growing, similar to the roles of paraprofessionals. It stands to reason that as paraprofessionals grow into and take on higher level work, librarians will be freed to take on higher level responsibilities as well. Professionals will have to spend more time on the big picture (Ramsay 2005). While having to fit in an increasing supervisory role, technical services administrators have had to do more staff training and spend more time on tools (Lewis 2005). Respondents felt that they needed to carve out additional time in their daily schedules to deal with an influx of more vendors in their area.

- **Some problems discussed or expressed seemed to be trends that are felt field-wide, not in technical services alone.** One librarian complained of not being seen as necessary anymore because users can get the information they need on their own. This has become a fear that resonates throughout the library field, as library users flock to Google for all the answers and come up with the conclusion that all their information needs can be met on the Internet. The information found on Google often contains great discrepancies that have been difficult to resolve, thus causing difficulties for library staff and patrons alike. So much information is available that it has become unwieldy and confusing to patrons, who have no conception of what is authoritative and what is not. Educating the community is seen as the librarian's responsibility ("yet not always welcome") (Ramsay 2005).

- **Participants were experiencing increased confrontation with legal issues in the realm of electronic resources.** Participants discussed the intensified work with licensing issues, legal contracts, proxy access, and consortial negotiations. These aspects of technical services become amorphous and other issues, such as copyright, become obscured. The legal and technical aspects of acquiring electronic material were overall perceived as a negative. Survey participants found that the additional responsibility relating to budgets, especially when it came to electronic resources, made for a far more complex and difficult path than when only the print format was involved. There was mention of how difficult it was to predict and track budgets, with factors such as annual fees, free with print, and print with added online subscriptions mentioned. There is a need to balance the big picture while maintaining attentiveness to details.

- **Those who saw more change for themselves within five years foresaw a broadening of their roles and a needed broadening of their understanding of the field.** One administrator voiced a need for the larger picture in comprehending the progress of the library field. Some did not foresee much change; these people already painted their own roles with broad strokes. One librarian stated that the role of the technical services librarian is to anticipate and prepare for the challenges of a rapidly changing field.

- **Leadership, vision, and communication will affect how technical services units will progress.** Several respondents stated that leadership, vision, and facilitation of communication were important factors in the future of technical services. Such skills have become requirements so that technical services departments can provide useful products and services to patrons. During the past few years, technical services units have had an even greater role in assisting public services in libraries (Bierman 2005). Successful organization and management of technical services units have led to technical services administrators needing such skills as the abilities to communicate, facilitate, and provide resources for staff. Others saw that their skills in organizational development played an important part in how their units grew. Continuing education in this area, therefore, is important to develop the skill sets of technical services administrators.

Discussion

After reviewing the various comments, it can be concluded that great change is occurring in technical services departments. There was a feeling among the respondents that the fast pace of everyday events and workflows will only increase over time. The responses indicated that future developments will take administrators to a different, and hopefully higher, level in the realm of organizational change. The burgeoning tidal wave of information is overwhelming. Such over-abundance will have a huge impact on the professional librarian in technical services units. Administrators in technical services departments will have to step up to a role of making the best resources available to patrons.

The survey respondents saw paraprofessionals assuming more and more of the routine tasks in technical services. Survey respondents had mixed feelings about faculty status. Some believed that academic librarians should not be faculty, especially in technical services, because the demands that come with this (publishing) may interfere with their work.

Conclusion

Possible follow-up studies can be done on emerging technologies, including the impact of Google, I books/WebCT, and other kinds of electronic/digital changes on technical services. Most patrons begin their searches by looking for information on Google. There should be a way to incorporate such research on this trend along with further studies on the decreasing use of the online catalog. Technical services departments will have to change their organizational structure and procedures in response to the impact of technological change. Some respondents, reflecting on recent studies in the field, have suggested that of the current librarians in technical services departments, over half plan to retire by the year 2010. Management of units will be passed to the next generation of librarians.

Many libraries will be prompted to outsource their cataloging and other types of time-consuming technical services processes. Outsourcing will become the norm in the coming years. There will be growth and hiring of additional personnel to work in the realm of electronic resources management. With the rapid growth and continual changes in the world of electronic resources, technical services administrators will have to continue exercising insightful leadership so that they can provide useful products for the libraries' users. There will be an even greater role shared by both technical and public services units so that electronic resources can be delivered effectively to customers.

The amount of electronic information continues to grow exponentially, while the need remains for administrators to adhere to budget constraints and cost-effectiveness. To manage their units efficiently, respondents indicated that they would need to learn about new and forthcoming technologies and more about organizational development. Although the survey respondents found both positive and negative aspects in their work, overall they were happy with the changing roles in the profession. Despite all the legal problems impinging on the technical aspects of acquiring and processing online materials, there is hope for a bright future.

References

Allen, Nancy H., and James F. Williams. 1995. The future of technical services: An administrative perspective. *Advances in Librarianship* 19: 59–89.

Bierman, Ken. 2005. Personal communication, November 22.

Bloss, Alex, and Don Lanier. 1997. The library department head in the context of matrix management and reengineering. *College & Research Libraries* 58 (November): 499–508.

Calhoun, Karen. 2003. Technology, productivity and change in library technical services. *Library Collections Acquisitions and Technical Services* 27 (3): 281–89.

Eden, Bradford Lee, ed. 2004. *Innovative Redesign and Reorganization of Library Technical Services.* Westport, CT: Libraries Unlimited.

Lewis, Linda K. 2005. Personal communication, September 12.

Medeiros, Norm. 2005. Factors influencing competency perceptions and expectations of technical services administrators. *LRTS* 49 (July): 167–74.

Mitchell, Marilyn, ed. 2007. *Library workflow redesign: Six case studies.* Washington, DC: Council on Library and Information Resources.

Mueller, Susan. 2005. Personal communication, November 7.

Nuzzo, David. 2005. Personal communication, September 2.

Ramsay, Karen. 2005. Personal communication, September 16.

Reese, Terry. 2007. *Terry's worklog*, March 24. Available at oregonstate.edu/~reeset/blog/archives/427.

Smith, Vicki Toy, and Kathryn Etcheverria. 2004. Staffing trends in academic library technical services. In *Innovative redesign and reorganization of library technical services,* ed. Bradford Lee Eden. Westport, CT: Libraries Unlimited.

Note: The author would like to thank Kathryn Etcheverria, Araby Greene, and Paoshan Yue for their encouragement and support. Araby Greene is Web development librarian and Paoshan Yue is director of technical services at the University of Nevada, Reno. Kathryn Etcheverria is state publications librarian at the Nevada State Library and Archives.

Appendix to Chapter 8: Technical Services Survey

1. In your library, technical services includes (check all that apply):
    ☐ Order processing   ☐ Serials processing   ☐ Electronic resources
    ☐ Cataloging   ☐ Marking   ☐ Interlibrary loan
    ☐ Other. Please specify_____

2. What is the size of your technical services unit (FTE; include students, part-time, full-time, all paid employees)?
    ☐ 1–4 ☐ 5–10   ☐ 11–15 ☐ 16–20 ☐ 21–25 ☐ 26 or more

3. Your technical services unit has had a net increase or decrease (FTE) of staff in the past:

    5 years: Increased: ☐1–2 ☐3–4 ☐5–6 ☐7–8 ☐ more–how many? _____
                Decreased: ☐1–2 ☐3–4 ☐5–6 ☐7–8 ☐ more–how many? _____

    10 years: Increased: ☐1–2 ☐3–4 ☐5–6 ☐7–8 ☐ more–how many? _____
                Decreased: ☐1–2 ☐3–4 ☐5–6 ☐7–8 ☐ more–how many? _____

4. In the past 10 years, these categories of staff have had a net increase or decrease (FTE)

    Professional: Increased: ☐1–2 ☐ 3–4 ☐ 5–6 ☐7–8 ☐ more–how many?___
                     Decreased: ☐1–2 ☐ 3–4 ☐5–6 ☐7–8 ☐ more–how many?___

    Paraprofessional: Increased: ☐1–2 ☐ 3–4 ☐ 5–6 ☐7–8 ☐ more–how many?___
                     Decreased: ☐1–2 ☐ 3–4 ☐5–6 ☐7–8 ☐ more–how many?___

5. What is your position (check all that apply)?
    ☐ Professional   ☐ Paraprofessional   ☐ Cataloging Supervisor
    ☐ Acquisitions Supervisor   ☐ Serials Supervisor
    ☐ Electronic Resources Supervisor ☐ Other. Please specify:_____

6. The number of years of your work experience in libraries is as follows:
    In this library: ☐0–5 ☐6–10   ☐11–15 ☐16–20 ☐21 or more
    Total experience: ☐0–5 ☐6–10   ☐11–15 ☐16–20 ☐21 or more

7. Consider the roles/job descriptions of professionals in your technical services unit. In the last 10 years their roles have:
    ☐ Grown larger in scope/responsibility
    ☐ Grown smaller in scope/responsibility
    ☐ Shifted to other areas   ☐ Not changed

8. If the roles of professionals have grown larger, their new responsibilities are:
    ☐ Moved from other library departments
    ☐ New to the library

9. In the last 10 years, the work loads of professionals have:

    ☐ Grown larger   ☐ Grown smaller   ☐ Not changed

10. If roles of professionals have changed, professionals have become (check all that apply):

    ☐ More viable in the job market   ☐ Less viable in the job market
    ☐ More valuable to the library   ☐ Less valuable to the library

11. Consider the roles/job descriptions of paraprofessionals in your technical services unit. In the last 10 years their roles have:

    ☐ Grown larger in scope/responsibility
    ☐ Grown smaller in scope/responsibility
    ☐ Shifted to other areas   Not changed

12. If the roles of paraprofessionals have grown larger, their new responsibilities are:

    ☐ Moved from other library departments   ☐ New to the library

13. In the last 10 years, the work loads of paraprofessionals have:

    ☐ Grown larger   ☐ Grown smaller   ☐ Not changed

14. If roles have changed, paraprofessionals have become (check all that apply):

    ☐ More viable in the job market   ☐ Less viable in the job market
    ☐ More valuable to the library   ☐ Less valuable to the library

15. When you think about staffing changes in your technical services unit, you feel (check all that apply):

    ☐ satisfied   ☐ dissatisfied   ☐ indifferent
    ☐ angry   ☐ confused   ☐ fearful
    ☐ resentful   ☐ thankful   ☐ joyful
    ☐ sad   ☐ other, please specify _____

16. Would you be willing to participate in an in-depth interview exploring further aspects of staffing in your library and your experiences/observations regarding staffing?

9

Library 2.0 and Technical Services: An Urban, Bilingual Community College Experience

Elisabeth Tappeiner

Kate Lyons

Web 2.0 enables organizations to leverage users of online resources as creators of content and value. In the e-commerce context, consumers use Web 2.0 applications to add value to a commercial Web site by contributing content such as product reviews. To a large extent, businesses enlist the help of consumers to sell their products. Academic libraries support a community of students and faculty in their educational and personal development and implementing new social technologies must draw upon the knowledge of the community to achieve these goals. Technology has often been used to deliver information in one direction: from librarian to patron. Library 2.0, which values collaboration and participation, creates a forum for two-way communication that draws upon the expertise of all users: faculty, students, and other librarians. A Library 2.0-inspired Web site is more than an interface with a library's catalog, databases, and selected Web resources; it is a forum for discussion and participation that benefits from patrons' contributions that enhance a library's online presence, making it a dynamic reflection of the community it serves.

The notion of the added value of participation can also apply to the work of technical services in libraries. Earlier discussions of reorganizing technical services, and library services in general, focused on redistributing staff and redesigning workflow in the context of shrinking resources. It is unrealistic to expect funding and staffing levels to improve, and libraries have invested resources in integrated library systems that do not currently provide Web 2.0 functionality. New technology-based tools, however, provide an opening to shift the focus from scarcity and limits to expanded, more integrated roles for technical services within the library.

In *Innovative Redesign and Reorganization of Library Technical Services*, Brad Eden discussed the "'McDonaldization' of the library profession [with] a focus on providing service and customer satisfaction both in the library schools and in the libraries rather than on building of collections or the organization and description of information, as in previous decades" (2004, ix). Library Web services tend to be focused on services that support reference and instruction, such as virtual reference, virtual library tours, and Web sites that highlight services rather than collections. As a result, the Web site has become the domain of public services, where even its collections of online resources—locally created pathfinders, collections of links to recommended Web sites, collections of digitized texts and images, and lists of databases and e-journals—are organized and displayed without input from catalogers.

This chapter is the result of collaboration between a technical services librarian and an information technology librarian, who were inspired by the potential of Library 2.0 to deepen and expand the notion of online access to information in a small academic library. It investigates the use of collaborative and community-building tools that characterize Library 2.0 to improve organization of and access to online resources, to generate community-centered discussion around collections, and ultimately to build collections that better reflect the needs and interests of the Eugenio María de Hostos Community College Library's user communities.

Web 2.0 and Library 2.0: An Interpretation

The concept of Web 2.0 was first articulated in the professional technology literature in 2002, and more recently, professional library literature has debated its implications for the library environment. The goal of this chapter is not to revisit this discussion of its value, but to identify core Web 2.0 principles and emerging Web-based applications and examine how they can be implemented in a small community college library to improve access to collections. In his seminal article on the subject, Tim O'Reilly (argues that Web 2.0 applications create an " 'architecture of participation' a built-in ethic of cooperation, in which the service acts primarily as an intelligent broker, connecting the edges to each other and harnessing the power of users themselves." Web 2.0 applications encourage participation and collaboration and value the knowledge of individual users; these core principles are aligned with the mission and culture of the Hostos Community College library.

Web 2.0 is as much a set of cultural values as it a set of technologies. "Openness and microcontent combine into a larger conceptual strand of Web 2.0, one that sees users as playing more of a foundational role in information architecture. Drawing on the "wisdom of crowds" argument, Web 2.0 services respond more deeply to users than Web 1.0 services" (Alexander 2007, 34). Web

2.0 provides new software tools that encourage participation, harness users' knowledge, and gather feedback from them more systematically.

Discussions of how Web 2.0 principles could and should be applied in the context of libraries have led to the concept of Library 2.0. The term entered discussions, mostly on blogs and listservs, in the fall of 2005 and was more formally introduced at the 2005 Internet Librarian conference. Immediately preceding and following the conference, in a flood of commentary about its definition, and its value, some librarians embraced the idea and others were critical of the new phrase. For an enlightening and thorough analysis of the contested meanings of Library 2.0, see the midwinter 2006 issue of *Cites and Insights* (Crawford). This chapter avoids these controversies and focuses instead on how practices and values commonly associated with Library 2.0—user feedback and collaboration, for example—can be used to integrate the expertise of technical services staff into public services areas of the Hostos Community College library. In a blog entry from January 2006, John Blyberg, currently the head of technology and digital initiatives at Darien Library, Connecticut, writes:

> The type of change L2 requires involves shifting focus from departments who previously bore the brunt of the public face of librarianship. For example, your IT departments (if you had one) were traditionally support mechanisms that kept the cogs turning behind the scenes. Increasingly, they are becoming an important part of the decision-making process and have more influence over how the public perceives your organization. As such, the type of people you hire into those position changes because the requirements are very different. L2 is going to require a great deal of inter-departmental integration. In order to be adept at navigating L2 waters, the old fiefdoms need to disappear. L2 requires drastic and sweeping changes to our internal cultures and will require some form of institutional enlightenment.

Users' expectations are changing, and librarians' skill sets, interests, and strengths are changing. Rather than the traditional departmental restructuring, as Blyberg writes, "L2 is going to require a great deal of inter-departmental integration." If a library embraces technology that improves communication, roles and teams can be more fluid. There is less need for restructuring in a library without deeply defined structures, where employees change, adapt, and learn.

Cataloger Richard Murray (2007) offers an unflattering stereotype of a cataloger: "On the rare occasion he or she is let out of the dungeon, it's to be the one at meetings who speaks in unintelligible MARC-ese about 'non-filing characters' and 'second indicator blank' and 'space colon space.' The cataloger's role in the library is to enforce rules that nobody understands and to make things as difficult as possible for everyone involved. Right?" Technical services has the reputation of being the most insular unit of the library. To some extent, each unit of the library represents a separate "dungeon" in which librarians are isolated from the activities of their colleagues. Library 2.0 opens up possibilities for integration and librarywide collaboration. Change can mean involving acquisitions librarians in promoting and generating discussion about new resources and reference librarians in providing consistent subject access to online resources, and it may require catalogers to translate LCSH-ese into a simple, straightforward set of rules for tagging and organizing Web links.

Finally, Stephen Abram (2005), vice president of innovation at SirsiDynix, frames Library 2.0 in the context of the user: "First and foremost, Librarian 2.0 understands his or her users at a deep level – not just as pointers and clickers. Librarian 2.0 understands end users deeply in terms of their goals and aspirations, workflows, social and content needs, and more. Librarian 2.0 is where the user is, when the user is there. This is an immersion environment that librarians are eminently qualified to contribute to." Library 2.0 technologies and practices bring librarians who perform a variety of functions closer to users. They call upon librarians to reevaluate and restructure traditional divisions of labor within the library with a view toward ensuring that librarians understand and respond to the needs of users in an informed and meaningful way.

Library 2.0: Implications for Hostos Community College

The mission of Hostos Community College is to offer access to higher education leading to intellectual growth and socioeconomic mobility through the development of linguistic, mathematical, technological, and critical thinking proficiencies needed for lifelong learning and success in a variety of programs, including careers, liberal arts, transfer, and those professional programs leading to licensure. Located in the south Bronx, Hostos Community College draws a majority of students who are non-native English speakers and traditionally underserved. It is the library's mission to support the college in serving this nontraditional, urban college community. Hostos strives to meet students where they are, linguistically and academically, and provide the education and support they need to move on to a four-year college or to graduate with a technical degree.

According to the Office of Institutional Research, the average age of the student body in 2006 was twenty-seven. Seventy-nine percent of Hostos's students are twenty-nine or younger. Although many students are part of the "Net Generation," born in the 1980s or later, comfortable with technology, eager for social interaction and collaboration in learning, Hostos's demographic profile is complex. Situated in one of the poorest congressional districts in the country, it draws students from area schools as well as countries in Latin America, Africa, and the Caribbean. As a provider of information and access to technology, the library seeks to meet students on their own terms and then provide them with skills for success as they continue their education and join the workforce.

The technical services department at the Hostos Library oversees acquisitions, some cataloging, serials, collection development, and electronic resources (including subject links on the library's Web site). Most of the cataloging has been outsourced to vendors, and library staff catalog special formats and perform quality control. The department consists of two full-time faculty members, a full-time paraprofessional, and two half-time support staff members.

Collection development is a collaborative process at Hostos Library, with each librarian assigned an academic department or unit. In their roles as departmental liaisons, librarians are aware of curricular developments, faculty interests, and general information needs of the departments and select books, journals, electronic resources, and Web links accordingly. The technical services department supports the relationships between the library faculty liaisons and teaching departments by ensuring that the liaisons have the best answers about collections and can order needed materials.

Although the technical services librarians spend some time working directly with students, either at the reference desk or through instruction, they do not primarily work one-on-one with students. Integrating participatory tools that characterize Library 2.0, however, may break down traditional barriers that separate technical and public services. Every librarian who works in collection development participates in organizing and indexing the collection. Also, technical services librarians serve as readers' advisors and provide virtual outreach to students and faculty about library collections.

Social Bookmarking, Tagging, and Folksonomy

> Tags are a simple way to categorize books according to how you think of them, not how some official librarian does.—LibraryThing

> Tags are one-word descriptors that you can assign to your bookmarks on del.icio.us to help you organize and remember them. Tags are a little bit like keywords, but they're chosen by you, and they do not form a hierarchy. You can assign as many tags to a bookmark as you like and rename or delete the tags later. So, tagging can be a lot easier and more flexible than fitting your information into preconceived categories or folders.—del.icio.us

Proponents of tagging often set up an "us" (antiauthoritarian, nonhierarchical, unofficial, free-thinking) versus "them" (librarians, official, hierarchical, inflexible) dichotomy, ignoring the fundamental goals of classification and subject cataloging as it has been practiced in libraries for more than a century. Although the notions of tagging and folksonomy are central to the principles of Web and Library 2.0, the values upon which they are based are not new to librarianship. In his *Rules for a Dictionary Catalog*, first published in 1876, Charles Ammi Cutter identified the principle of the "convenience of the public."

He argued that in creating a system for access to materials "cataloguers should be concerned with 'the public's habitual way of looking at things' " (quoted. in Chan 1994, 160). Lois Chan goes on to describe the difficulty of following this principle:

> One cannot define user and usage because there is no such thing as a "typical library user." Patrons come into the library with different backgrounds and different purposes, and there has never been an objective way to determine how they approach the catalog, or what their purposes are. (1994, 160)

Catalogers have traditionally been responsible for expressing the subject, the "aboutness," of a work by choosing subject terms from controlled vocabularies such as *Library of Congress Subject Headings*, but are always mindful that these systems only approximate "the public's habitual way of looking at things." User added tags, or natural language keywords, and social software are technological innovations that support the principles that Cutter identified over a century ago. Social software lets users describe "how they look at things," and more important, their tags improve access for other users.

Many Web 2.0 proponents consider tagging and folksonomies as necessary antidotes to the hierarchical nature and inflexibility of controlled vocabularies. Groups of users with similar interests may use similar tags, creating flat and democratic folksonomies as opposed to a hierarchical controlled vocabulary. In an interview with Lee Rainie (2007), director of Pew Internet and American Life Project, David Weinberger stated:

> Tagging also allows social groups to form around similarities of interests and points of view. If you're using the same tags as I do, we probably share some deep commonalities.... And, by looking over the public field of tags, we can see which tags are most frequently used and how they relate. Those patterns are called "folksonomies"—it's a play on the word "taxonomies." Folksonomies reveal how the public is making sense of things, not just how expert cataloguers think we ought to be thinking.

Folksonomies may include tags for concepts and terms that may have evolved recently, such as words that describe new and emerging technologies. This flexibility is also valuable in a bilingual environment in which the folksonomies might include terms from various languages. The characterization of catalogers as experts who decide how they ought to think, however, is unfair to those who have long grappled with the difficulties of creating subject access for unknown others. In addition, a glance at the practice of tagging on popular social bookmarking sites (such as del.icio.us or flickr.com) reveals the familiar problems of inconsistency and ambiguity. Even small groups of like-minded individuals do not agree on tags and terminology. In many contexts, they don't have to. But in an academic library, where tags describe specific courses, academic disciplines within the institutional organization, or types of resources, some level of vocabulary control is necessary for consistency and resource discovery.

In an ideal information retrieval world, the metadata that catalogers use to describe materials in a collection and the subjects and keywords users enter as search terms would be identical. In the real world, catalogers' sense of users' search habits, combined with reference librarians and information literacy instruction, is what makes information retrieval work. With Library 2.0 tools, "revealing how the public is making sense of things" makes expert catalogers even more successful. Looking at how users are tagging their collections leads to ideas for reorganizing collections and expanding controlled vocabularies. Their tags provide valuable insight into how they think about and search for information. In an environment in which many students are working toward proficiency in English, social bookmarking and folksonomies provide another context for language learning. Students can look at a Web site and the various tags used to describe it, many of them synonyms that range from formal academic vocabulary to slang or jargon.

Social bookmarking sites also allow for new and intuitive methods of displaying subject terms. Tag clouds are visual representations of the tags used to describe resources. Each tag in the cloud is a link to the resources in the collection tagged with that word. Tags appear in a font size that correlates with their frequency of use, so that tags used most often to index a collection appear in the largest font. A tag cloud can display in alphabetical order or randomly. The organizing principle is size (frequency of use) rather than a predetermined hierarchy. Sometimes a number appears in parentheses next to the tag, to indicate the number of resources in the collection described by that tag. Users can easily scan the entire collection of tags in a cloud to get an overall sense of terms used and view their patterns of use.

For a cataloger creating a hybrid system that uses tags and controlled vocabulary that will be displayed in a tag cloud, it is important to determine which tags to display most prominently and to create rules for applying those tags. Popular examples of sites that use tag clouds are del.icio.us and flickr.com, a popular photo storage and sharing site. Tag clouds are also used to show patterns of vocabulary use in other contexts. The "US Presidential Speeches Tag Cloud" at Chirag Mehta's (2006) Web site (chir.ag/phernalia/preztags) shows the frequency of words used by U.S. presidents in their speeches over time, illustrating the concerns of different presidents at different historical moments.

In Practice: Tagging Web Resources Using Del.icio.us

Del.icio.us is a social bookmarking tool that embodies the possibilities of Library 2.0. Much like the favorites list in a browser, it stores a list of Web sites that a user wants to remember. However, where a favorites list in a browser only stores the URL and description, del.icio.us allows users to tag the Web site with their own descriptors, and because it's a Web-based tool, users can access the Web site from any Web browser. Social bookmarking enables users to share their bookmarks with other del.icio.us users and create their own mini-lists from other users' lists, mixing them up and retagging them with their own descriptors. Del.icio.us allows individuals to organize and access links and their associated tags and provides a forum to share and discover new resources.

The Hostos Community College Web site features a collection of subject links loosely associated with the academic departments and programs the college offers, as well as some online, freely available reference resources. The list was originally created in 2001 from the bookmarks a few faculty members saved on their Web browsers. Hostos librarians annotated the links and e-mailed them to the library's Webmaster along with instructions on which of the subjects to list the links under. The library Webmaster copied and pasted the links into a static HTML document. This document was becoming increasingly time-consuming to maintain and difficult to organize, and valuable information was lost among dead links and an inflexible system of organization.

To simplify the maintenance of these links and enhance resource discovery, the links were posted to del.icio.us to maintain and organize this collection. Because it was a popular social bookmarking site, the expectation was that a certain number of Hostos students were already familiar with del.icio.us. For others, this was an opportunity to introduce an organizational tool that enables students who may not necessarily own their own computers to keep track of and organize their "favorites" with a free online service accessible from anywhere. Also, it provides both a tag cloud and search feature that easily integrate into the library's Web page, enhancing browsabilty of the links. It enables those who can log into the library's account (currently librarians as well as some technical services staff members) to make changes, to tag and organize bookmarks in ways that make sense to students and faculty in various academic departments.

Del.icio.us is also a useful collection development tool. Once a link is added to the list of favorites, a user can see how many other accounts have linked to the same resources and view their links. For example, Hardin MD's list of radiation technology Web sites has been bookmarked by two other del.icio.us users who link to other similar sites. Del.icio.us is a tool that takes advantage of the specialized knowledge of each librarian to build and maintain a collection of links that is accessible and useful to students and faculty. The collection was developed by a community of librarians based on a simple controlled vocabulary, established by the technical services librarian and enhanced by tags added by specialists in every subject.

This project combines a simple controlled vocabulary based on the structure of academic departments within the college and the flexibility of tagging to create organized, user-friendly subject access to a wide range of Internet resources for the college community. In their roles as subject specialists, librarians tag subject links they post to del.icio.us. These links are organized by the technical services librarian into "bundles," or headings that group together related tags. The first bundles correspond to the college's academic departments: Allied Health, Behavioral, and Social Sciences; Business; English Language and Cognition (ESL); Library; Mathematics; and Natural Sciences. These terms reflect the departmental organization of the college and are familiar to faculty and students. In addition to the departmental bundles, bundles represent type of resource, place, and language. These roughly correspond to geographical and form *Library of Congress Subject Headings* subdivisions.

Although del.icio.us tags do not allow for faceted browsing, a user can perform a search that combines tags for subject "literature" and resource type "fulltext" to search for a link by subject and attribute. Any tag can be renamed or split into two tags, a simple form of authority control. Tags can also carry descriptions so that confusing tags—those referring to a particular assignment or class, for example—can be more fully described when users click on them.

When a librarian selects a new link to add to the library's list of favorites, she logs into del.icio.us and posts it. The URL is automatically filled in, and the selector then needs to add both a title and tags. Selectors are asked to look for an obvious title and are encouraged to consult with a technical services librarian when in doubt. Del.icio.us automatically displays tags that have already been used, providing useful suggestions and a sort of thesaurus. The rules for tagging are fairly simple:

- For each resource, include the name of at least one academic department or resource type to make departments display prominently in the tag cloud.

- If a link relates to a specific class or assignment, use the number indicated in the college catalog for the class and add the professor's name (e.g., ENG1101Smith).

Librarians are reminded to consider the following when tagging their links:

- In addition to subjects, what are other attributes of the resource? Is it used to find other resources? Is it an image or sound file? Did an organization or person create the resource? Is it associated with a place or time period?

- Use tags for variant spellings and synonyms (e.g., theater and theatre and drama)

- Does this resource have content in Spanish? Would tags in Spanish be appropriate?

Because students and other library users do not tag the links, the full potential of user-generated tags and the folksonomies they create is not realized. Only allowing library staff and faculty to tag resources maintains control of the list of subject links, which are selected specifically to support the curriculum of the college. Involving librarians in the tagging process, however, shifts the job of providing subject access to these links into the hands of subject specialists, who work closely with faculty and students in their subject areas. The simple controlled vocabulary and rules of application should encourage consistency. Students, faculty, and other users can access this collection from the static page on the library's Web site, which uses XML to display the links from del.icio.us (www.hostos.cuny.edu/library/hcc/subject-links.asp), and by visiting the library's del.icio.us account directly (del.icio.us/hostoslibrary).

Once the collection was tagged, the next step was deciding how to display the information to users. A priority was to link directly to the library's del.icio.us account for users who are already familiar with social bookmarking and, possibly, to introduce newcomers to del.icio.us. It also made sense to provide a more traditional search interface based on the Web forms elements, such as drop-down menus and text-boxes on the library's Web page. The drop-down box lists the academic departments at the college so that users can easily find the resources associated with their departments. The keyword search (textbox) searches tags. Finally, a tag cloud gives users a visual representation of the subject tags. Whenever a resource is added to del.icio.us and tagged, it is easily searchable using any of these methods. (See figure 9.1.)

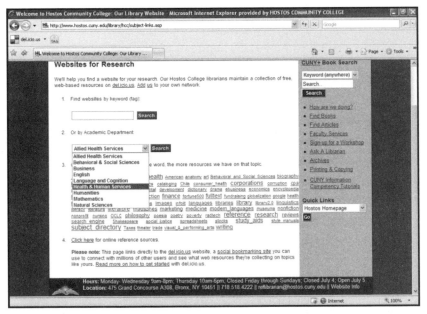

Figure 9.1. Screenshot of del.icio.us Search Page and Tag Cloud on the Hostos Community College Library Web Site.

The results of the del.icio.us search are displayed on the del.icio.us Web site. Although it is possible, making use of Web programming technology like

RSS and Javascript, to display the list of results on the library's Web site, one of the goals of using collaborative sites like del.icio.us is to be where students are. For those in the Hostos community who are already using del.icio.us, displaying the results on the familiar interface is intuitive. On her blog, librarian.net, Jessamyn West (2007) describes a Harvard professor's experience with their incoming class of undergraduates: "They did a show of hands survey of their incoming class to Harvard this year and asked who had a Facebook page. The answer wasn't 'most of them' but every single one of them." Although many Hostos students are on the "bridged" side of the digital divide, using technology on a regular basis and fitting the stereotypical profile of the Net Generation, Hostos serves students who do not necessarily have access to technology resources. Nevertheless, linking directly to del.icio.us from the library's Web site is a simple way to introduce new users to the social web. (See figure 9.2.)

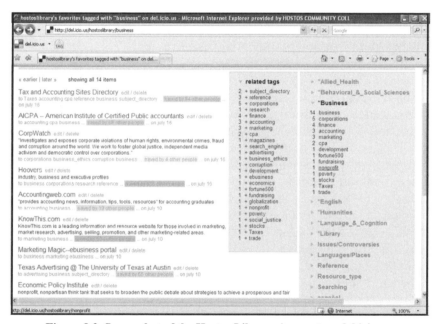

Figure 9.2. Screenshot of the Hostos Library Account on del.icio.us.

In Practice: Creating Community on LibraryThing

On many academic library Web sites, the presence of technical services is limited to a link to the OPAC and a list of new acquisitions. The Hostos Community College Library's Web site has both, but a priority was to integrate the Library 2.0 values of participation and community building describing and promoting collections. Librarians at Hostos are keenly aware that many students are being exposed to the intellectual and social value of all libraries for the first time. The library is the main venue on campus, both physical and virtual, for students to find information, collaborate, and share ideas. Another goal is to build collections that not only meet their academic needs but also stimulate curiosity and discussion. Students can come to the library to pick up a good novel, check out an interesting DVD, and, hopefully, talk about what they are thinking and reading with students and faculty. Library 2.0 can extend the physical collaborative space of the library to the online environment by creating a forum for online discussion about resources and get better feedback about collections from faculty and students. Facilitating the involvement of subject selectors in the promotion of new books was a priority because they chose the resources and are best equipped to discuss them with faculty and students. The Web 2.0 application for meeting these goals is LibraryThing.

LibraryThing describes itself as "an online service to help people catalog their books easily." It uses bibliographic information from various sources, including commercial Web sites, and MARC records created by selected research libraries, including the Library of Congress. As on del.icio.us, users sign up for a free online account, which they can access remotely. They can add books to their library, tag them, review them, and find other accounts with similar titles. Its social tools are even more developed, allowing users to join groups and book discussions and contribute to "talks," online discussions on a variety of topics, including librarianship and cataloging. It serves as a kind of readers' advisory, suggesting titles similar to those posted to a library, and it even has an "unsuggestor" for books that are least likely to appear in the same collections. LibraryThing allows users to add and share information about titles—functionalities that many librarians would love to see in OPACs. It also sends users out into a broader world of books and reading.

On the Hostos Library Web site, LibraryThing displays selected new acquisitions and highlights books from the collection related to an event (e.g., women's history month or a conference hosted by the college). Titles can be added to LibraryThing one at a time by selectors who want to highlight noteworthy titles or by importing any file containing ISBNs (e.g., a spreadsheet of new titles from a vendor or the results of an OPAC search for books on a given subject). Once a book is posted to a LibraryThing account, users can review it, tag it, and view other accounts that link to the same book. Titles can be displayed locally in various ways, through tag clouds, author clouds, or rotating lists of books. Once users click on a title, they are taken to the LibraryThing Web site, and local bibliographic control is lost. LibraryThing's first level display provides basic bibliographic information and book covers. Users can link to "social information," which includes reviews, links to other members with the book in their library, and tags. "Book information" provides complete bibliographic information and, in some cases, the MARC record. It is easy to add a link that takes users back to the library's local OPAC. (See figure 9.3.)

Figure 9.3. Screenshot of Hostos Library's Recommended Reading Page, Including a Feed from the Technical Services LibraryThing Account.

As of yet, no rules have been established for adding and tagging books in the "hostoslibrary" LibraryThing group, and any user who signs up for a LibraryThing account can join the Hostos group. The community of users is limited to Hostos librarians for posting online resources to del.icio.us, but any member of the Hostos Library group can contribute tags, reviews, or even titles to the Web site. LibraryThing provides an open forum for discussion about local collections and the world of books, and it is important to encourage participation by having has few barriers as possible.

LibraryThing is a commercial Web site that has capitalized on the fact that people love to organize their books and talk about them with others. Librarians have always known this, and a potentially richer source of virtual interaction about library collections is Worldcat.org, OCLC's contribution to Library 2.0, which allows registered users to add reviews and notes to WorldCat records and request items via ILL and links to local catalogs at the item level for easier access to call numbers and circulation status. Because it already contains the MARC records for millions for books, audiovisual, and electronic resources as well as holdings of member libraries around the world, it has the potential to become the LibraryThing for libraries. Nevertheless, LibraryThing offers richer opportunities for social interaction than WorldCat.org currently provides.

Traditionally, after librarians send requests to the acquisitions librarian, their job as selector is done. Technical services staff add a local field to the

MARC record when a book is cataloged to mark it as a new book for the new acquisitions list. Now, selectors are asked to choose at least a couple of books to promote, review, and tag on LibraryThing. If they are really successful, they may have to participate in a book discussion with students and outside participants. In essence, LibraryThing may generalize more of the work. It may take awhile before all librarians begin to use it, and a few may never participate. The goal in using LibraryThing is that a few active librarians and faculty will generate enough interest so that more and more members of the Hostos community will participate and integrate it into classes and assignments. Students are becoming increasingly used to this type of online interaction and sharing of information, and at least some will thrive in these online communities.

In Practice: Google Docs, Wikis, and Vendor Tools

Web 2.0 applications reflect the value of transparency in the workplace and flattening of hierarchies. The behind-the-scenes work of technical services is largely administrative, and practical Web 2.0 tools have helped with the daily work of the technical services department. In addition to ordering and cataloging materials, technical services staff keep statistics and communicate information about budgets and new titles to other librarians and administrators. Moreover, the work of technical services is collaborative. An item is handled by every staff member as it makes its way through the process of selection, ordering, receiving, cataloging, and processing. Clear and consistent communication and tracking are essential throughout this process. Saving departmental documents, such as statistics or training materials, on a single computer causes confusion and creates inconsistency. Google Docs and Spreadsheets offered a solution to the problem of sharing and updating departmental documents. Google Docs and Spreadsheets describes itself as "a free web-based word processing and spreadsheet program that keeps documents current and lets the people you choose update files from their own computers." Now the technical services department uses Google Docs (www.google.com/google-d-s/b1.html) to share files that track statistics for new materials, serials information, and withdrawn materials. Two or three people can work on any of these documents at the same time.

Another typical Web 2.0 tool helps the technical services department share and revise the departmental manual of operations, which is now a wiki posted on the free service, pbwiki.com. Now all department staff have access to the very latest manifestation of the fluid rules and procedures, which they can enhance and update themselves as policies evolve.

Discussion of Library 2.0 and vendors mostly focuses on OPACs, but technical services staff work with vendors of all types. Library vendors supply books, electronic resources, journals, supplies, and services, and more and more vendors are providing their clients in libraries with information about products and accounts that can be downloaded and manipulated. Although the ability to download an Excel file from a vendor's Web site may not exactly fall into the realm of Web 2.0, it is a step in a good direction. Some book vendors are creating Web sites that look more and more like Amazon—with reviews, sales rankings, lists of recommended titles, and book covers. Library vendors can use the same strategies as other commercial Web sites to draw from different sources, including the librarians they serve, to provide information for their customers.

Conclusion: Training, Buy-in, and Participation

Because the Technical Services Department is adopting technology whose success hinges on participation from other library staff as well as, ideally, the entire college community, it was crucial to take extra time at the beginning stages of this project to talk individually to staff and college faculty who are especially receptive to these ideas. Adopting Library 2.0 practices not only changes the workflow, policies, and procedures, but it is also a change in organizational culture.

Hostos Library has prioritized technology innovation in its strategic plan, and the administration encourages creative thinking and new ideas. In addition, most staff members are already comfortable with communicating by e-mail, searching the Internet, and using word processing and spreadsheet programs, and they are interested in learning about new technologies. Although it is unlikely that faculty who never use e-mail or the Internet will use LibraryThing or del.icio.us, hopefully enough librarians will participate to make these initiatives successful.

Reaching out to the entire college community and getting participation from faculty and students campuswide will be a real challenge. Nevertheless, the library's collection of del.icio.us subjects links is an improvement over the static HTML subject links page, and even if the college community never takes advantage of the social aspects of the site, the Technical Services Department has streamlined internal workflow. Likewise, wikis, Google Docs, and other online tools for shared projects and documents have simplified internal processes.

Technical services will benefit from integrating some Library 2.0 applications into workflow, and the department has begun to implement the changes outlined in this chapter. But this is only the first step. The true challenge will be to engage in an ongoing, open dialogue about various departmental roles; how to learn and adapt to change; and how to use technology to improve workflow and build meaningful community among librarians, staff, faculty, and students.

References

Abram, Stephen. 2005. Web 2.0, Library 2.0, and Librarian 2.0: Preparing for the 2.0 world. *SirsiDynix OneSource*. Available at www.imakenews.com/eletra/mod_print_view.cfm?this_id=505688&u=sirsi&issue_id=000101262. (accessed April 30, 2007).

Alexander, Bryan. 2007. A new wave of innovation for teaching and learning? *Educause Review* 41 (2). Academic Search Premier. EBSCO. Hostos Community College Lib. Available at web.ebscohost.com/ (accessed July 10, 2007).

Blyberg, John. 2006. 11 reasons why Library 2.0 exists and mMatters. *Blyberg.net*, January 1. Available at www.blyberg.net/2006/01/09/11-reasons-why-library-20-exists-and-matters (accessed July 16, 2007).

Chan, Lois Mai. 1994. *Cataloging and classification: An introduction.* 2nd ed. New York: McGraw-Hill.

Crawford, Walt. 2006. Library 2.0 and "Library 2.0". *Cites & Insights* 6 (2). Available at citesandinsights.info/civ6i2.pdf (accessed July 10, 2007).

Eden, Bradford Lee, ed. 2004. *Innovative redesign and reorganization of library technical services : Paths for the future and case studies.* Westport, CT: Libraries Unlimited.

Mehta, Chirag. 2006. US presidential speeches tag cloud. Available at chir.ag/phernalia/preztags/ (accessed July 18, 2007).

Murray, Richard. 2007. The whimsy of cataloging. *LISCareer.com* (June 14). Available at www.liscareer.com/murray_cataloging.htm (accessed September 4, 2008).

O'Reilly, Tim. 2005. What is Web 2.0? Design patterns and business models for the next generation of software. *Tim O'Reilly.com,* September 30. Available at www.oreillynet.com/pub/a/oreilly/tim/news/2005/09/30/what-is-web-20.html (accessed September 4, 2008).

Rainie, Lee. 2007. 28% of online Americans have used the Internet to tag content; forget Dewey and his decimals, Internet users are revolutionizing the way we classify information—and make sense of it. *The Pew Internet and American Life Project,* January 31. Available at www.pewinternet.org/pdfs/PIP_Tagging.pdf (accessed September 4, 2008).

West, Jessamyn. 2007. But once libraries get to facebook, what do they do there?" *librarian.net,* June 9. Available at www.librarian.net/stax/2062/but-once-libraries-get-to-facebook-what-do-they-do-there/ (accessed June 15, 2007).

10

Web 2.0 and Technical Services: Reorganizing Workflow around Collaborative Interfaces

Adam Murray

Introduction

Since the term "Web 2.0" was coined in 2004 by O'Reilly Media's Dale Dougherty, it has become much more than a title of a conference meant to showcase Web innovators, as originally intended. "Web 2.0" has become the accepted title of the next generation of the Web. Many view the principles behind Web 2.0 as the natural evolution of online activity. Hugely successful Web sites have sprung up—seemingly overnight—that capitalize on the network effects of Web 2.0 technology, while existing online retailers have rushed to make their content more dynamic by allowing for greater interactivity between sites and customers. An entirely new business model, incorporating the notions of the "long tail," user-generated content, and the Internet-as-platform has emerged, changing the ways in which online businesses turn a profit.

Outside of the corporate sector, many libraries have seized Web 2.0 technology, hoping to utilize its principles to increase service to users. Despite being the genesis of such rapid change, Web 2.0 remains an enigma for many. What is Web 2.0? How can libraries—specifically technical services—make use of Web 2.0 technology? What changes have to be made to technical services workflow to accommodate this new technology? This chapter examines the answers to these questions by adopting O'Reilly Media's *Web 2.0 Principles and Best Practices* (Musser 2007) as a framework of study. These principles identify the factors that constitute Web 2.0 technology and provide a valuable lens through which we can examine the innovations put into place in the technical services area of one academic university library system. Readers of this chapter will gain not only an understanding of what Web 2.0 technology is, but also insight into the possible ways it can be used in technical services, as well as the issues of implementing the technology into an existing workflow.

Literature Review

A review of professional library literature reveals the degree to which Web 2.0 has become an important topic of discussion. Closer inspection shows that very few articles address Web 2.0 in technical services. The majority of articles appear to fall within four broad categories (arranged in order of prevalence):

• What is Web 2.0?

• Implementing Web 2.0 technology in public services

• Technical specifics of developing and using Web 2.0 technology

• Cataloging, tagging, and folksonomies

Under the "What is Web 2.0?" trend are articles attempting to detail the components of Web 2.0 and what Web sites are the most popular/promising Web 2.0 sites. Examples of this type of article are Stephens (2006), Dubon (2006), and Dye (2007). Notess's (2006a) article highlights the extent of anxiety present in the library profession about adopting Web 2.0 philosophies.

The second most prevalent trend in library literature is about the implementation of Web 2.0 technology in public service areas, especially in public libraries and school media centers. Bolan et al.'s (2007) and Hauser's (2007) articles are evidence of this trend, and how many libraries are concerned with utilizing Web 2.0 technology to draw children and teens into library activities.

The technical demands and requirements of implementing Web 2.0 technology represent the next most populous trend in library literature. Notess's (2006b) article examines the increasingly numerous markup language choices available for use in Web 2.0 Web sites, whereas Coombs (2007) looks at how factors of Web 2.0 philosophy were taken into account during a redesign of an academic library's Web site. A final example is Huffman's (2006) article on the practical implementation of RSS feeds, podcasts, and wikis for National Geographic's Libraries & Information Services.

The last trend of note in library literature regarding Web 2.0 includes articles looking at folksonomies and tagging. Kemp's (2007) article looks at how interactive Web sites and user expectations of tagging capabilities may have an impact on the future of cataloging. Szomszor et al. (2007) explore the possibility of utilizing user-generated tags or keywords to predict user interest in movies with similar tags.

Although there are many articles in professional library literature dealing with Web 2.0, none of the major trends examines the ways in which Web 2.0 technology may be utilized by technical services areas.

Case Study

This case study looks at the application of Web 2.0 technology in a single university library technical services department and explores three questions:

- What is Web 2.0?

- How can libraries—specifically technical services—make use of Web 2.0 technology?

- What changes have to be made to technical services workflow to accommodate this new technology?

Conducting this examination in the form of a case study is essential to provide readers with a clear understanding of the actions and rationale preceding, during, and following a new workflow implementation. It is equally critical that this case study be viewed through an analytic framework, allowing readers to extrapolate from the actions of the single university library to their own institution.

The structure of the case study is an explanation of the analytic framework, a brief institutional profile, and an examination of the application of the analytic framework to the institution.

Analytic Framework: *Web 2.0 Principles and Best Practices*

This case study is framed using the *Web 2.0 Principles and Best Practices* outlined by O'Reilly Media's John Musser (2007). As mentioned previously, the term "Web 2.0" was first coined by a member of the O'Reilly Media Group, which defines Web 2.0 as "a set of economic, social, and technology trends that collectively form the basis for the next generation of the Internet—a more mature, distinctive medium characterized by user participation, openness, and network effects" (Musser 2007, 12). Since then, the phrase—and O'Reilly's definition of Web 2.0—has become accepted worldwide. Web 2.0 is more complex, however, than simply the next generation or the natural evolution of the Internet. As Musser (2007, 12) states, "it is the underlying patterns that are much more important than a definition." Identifying and describing these "underlying patterns" will answer this chapter's first question, "what is Web 2.0?" and provide a framework through which one can analyze the implementation of Web 2.0 technology in library technical services.

The *Web 2.0 Principles and Best Practices* give a clear definition of Web 2.0 by describing its components (Musser 2007, 12):

> - Harnessing collective intelligence: create an architecture of participation that uses network effects to move from "one-to-many publishing" towards "many-to-many" publishing

- Data [are] the next "Intel Inside": use unique data sources

- Innovation in assembly: build platforms . . . where remixing of data and services creates new opportunities and markets

- Rich user experiences: go beyond traditional web-page metaphors to deliver rich user experiences combining the best of desktop and on-line software

- Software above the level of a single device: create software that spans Internet-connected devices and builds on the growing pervasiveness of online experience

- Perpetual beta: move away from old models of software development and adoption in favor of online, continuously updated software as a service model

- Leveraging the long tail: capture niche markets profitably through the low-cost economics and broad reach enabled by the Internet

- Lightweight models and cost-effective scalability: use lightweight business- and software-development models to build products and businesses quickly and cost-effectively

The *Web 2.0 Principles and Best Practices* outline the overall components of Web 2.0 in all its variety of uses. Several of the *Web 2.0 Principles and Best Practices* are aimed at creating and sustaining a business using Web 2.0 technology. To adapt the *Web 2.0 Principles and Best Practices* to the focus of this chapter, three of the components were not utilized. "Harnessing collective intelligence" and "software above the level of a single device" were deemed too similar to warrant separate analysis and were therefore combined; by the very nature of harnessing collective intelligence, it is required that technical services faculty and staff utilize software above the level of a single Internet-connected device. Maintaining a state of perpetual beta by adopting new software on a constant basis proves inefficient for technical services, due to the necessity of providing training opportunities for faculty/staff and library users. Although technical services may have several of its own long-tails, such as a backlog of materials for cataloging or a backlog of orders for out-of-print books, faculty/staff efforts regarding these long-tails are predominantly aimed at eliminating them, rather than capitalizing on them as the traditional business model of the long-tail is prone to do. Web 2.0 technology may have the potential to affect this long-tail elimination, but this is not its primary purpose.

Musser also outlines some of the issues and problems associated with each of the *Web 2.0 Principles and Best Practices*. Of these, privacy of the individual and of the provider are foremost, followed by issues of information control brought about by the decentralized workflow structure necessitated by the harnessing of collective intelligence. Specifics of these issues are discussed more fully within the context of adapting Web 2.0 technology to library technical service workflows below.

The *Web 2.0 Principles and Best Practices* are used to anchor the case study's examination of the innovations taking place at a single university library with the accepted vision of Web 2.0 as put forth by those who first named the phenomenon. Grounding this case study of a single library's utilization of Web 2.0 technology in an analytic framework is critical to allow readers to extrapolate from the single instance to their own institutions.

Institutional Profile

This chapter looks into the steps taken by the technical services area of one academic university library system—Murray State University—to implement various Web 2.0 technologies. The initial consideration of these technologies resulted from a recognition of various information needs in the library and the general university community. A search for possible solutions to these information needs led the author to develop a procedure based on Web 2.0 technology that was integrated into the existing workflows. To place the adoption of these procedures in a context useful to the readers, it is necessary to provide a profile of the university, library, and technical services department prior to the implementation.

Murray State University Libraries serves a comprehensive university, consisting of approximately 8,800 full-time equivalent students. The academic community of the university is divided into six colleges: Agriculture, Business and Public Affairs, Education, Health Sciences and Human Services, Humanities and Fine Arts, and Science Engineering. Each of these colleges is further subdivided into academic departments, for example, Biology, Chemistry, Engineering and Physics, Geosciences, Industrial and Engineering Technology, and Mathematics and Statistics operate under the College of Science and Engineering. Within each department a faculty member is designated to serve as a department representative to the University Libraries. This department representative is responsible for requesting and passing along other faculty members' requests for specific titles to Acquisitions to expend the department's library materials allocation. The library materials allocations are intended to support one-time purchases, such as books, DVDs, and CDs. Each department's allocation is calculated by applying a formula that factors in student enrollment, the number of faculty members in the department, and the average cost of materials for that subject.

A system of deadlines requires that each department representative submit requests sufficient to expend certain percentages of their allocations by certain points of the academic year. Any of the allocations not accounted for by requests at each deadline can be reallocated by the dean of University Libraries. The possibility of losing any of the library materials allocation results in intense interest in the expenditure of funds by department chairs and college deans. It is therefore essential that department representatives, department chairs, and college deans have up-to-date account information detailing the totals of materials that are either "not yet ordered," "on order," or "received." Department representatives have the additional requirement of needing to know the status of individual titles in the order process, to provide updates to the faculty of their departments.

Initially, these differing information needs were met by the Acquisitions unit through a series of monthly printed reports. These reports were color-coded to assist in their interpretation; for example, total account expenditures and encumbrances were printed on green paper, while the individual titles of those materials that had been received in the past month were printed on yellow paper. Providing these reports, specifically tailored to detail the activity of individual departments, proved logistically very difficult. Sorting the information on a monthly basis was not in itself problematic, as reports based on the activity of the integrated library system (ILS) were created that arranged the information in an orderly way. As the ILS did not include a Web-based reporting function, however, distributing the information to various people—all of whom required configurations of information—proved difficult. For example, deans only got the green reports, while department chairs received both the green and blue reports; department representatives were sent all reports. Despite being color-coded, the reports provided so much information they proved confusing to many department representatives. The challenge of meeting these information requirements in a more time-sensitive and unambiguous manner provided the impetuous for developing a new workflow that would both serve the information needs of the department representatives, chairs, and deans and remain logistically feasible for the faculty and staff of the libraries' Acquisitions unit.

Application

The author conceptualized such a workflow—one that satisfied the various information needs of the university community as well as the Acquisitions unit's need for efficiency—as a portal. This "one-stop shopping" destination would have to provide widely different types of information, recombined in patterns that addressed the specific information needs of various faculty and staff. Determining the information needs of deans, department chairs, and department representatives was accomplished on a trial-and-error basis through the design and distribution of the unit's color-coded monthly reports. Feedback from all levels of administration was provided to the author, allowing him to develop a clearer understanding of their needs.

Making this "portal" Web-based was originally suggested by one of the department representatives. A Web-based platform had the potential of providing constantly updated information to any Internet-connected device in the world, replacing the color-coded paper reports, which were delivered monthly (and were rendered obsolete almost immediately by ongoing Acquisitions activity).

Some ILSs provide such Web-based platforms for this very purpose; however, the ILS utilized by Murray State University Libraries does not possess such capabilities.

After some initial conversations with the Systems unit of the libraries, the author concluded that, although a fully developed program or software would be wonderful to implement, the necessity of having a simple and cheap system that could be put into operation relatively quickly took a higher priority. From this conclusion, the author turned to Web 2.0 technology, which would make the delivery of recombined information to the university community an efficient process for the Acquisitions unit. The two Web 2.0 technologies most specifically utilized were Google Docs and Spreadsheets, for providing fiscal and order status information, and LibraryThing for communicating material selection suggestions based on similar collections. Google Docs and Spreadsheets is a Web-based word processor/spreadsheet function that allows the document or spreadsheet's creator to invite other people to use the file. Once they accept the invitation, all invitees are allowed to edit information simultaneously. LibraryThing is "an online service to help people catalog their books easily . . . LibraryThing also connects people with the same books, comes up with suggestions for what to read next, and so on" (*About LibraryThing* 2007).

Following is an analysis of the development of an information portal via the spreadsheet function in Google Docs and Spreadsheets. Each of the adopted *Web 2.0 Principles and Best Practices* is explored individually.

Harnessing collective intelligence: "Web 2.0 reflects the maturation of the Internet as a communications medium, one that is user-centered, decentralized, and collaborative" (Musser 2007, 15). One of the aspects of providing information to the university community via monthly paper reports was the overwhelming logistical problem of sorting the information into reports appropriate for the different needs of the faculty. This arose from a dilemma in organizing the workflow around the generation of the reports. The author was forced either to interrupt Acquisitions activities to produce the reports in a timely manner or to assign the entire task to one person. Either option was inefficient, resulting in out-of-date information being distributed to the deans, department chairs, and department representatives.

The spreadsheet function of Google Docs and Spreadsheets allows for the decentralization of this reporting procedure. The four most important reports distributed in the color-coded monthly packets could be streamlined into department-specific spreadsheets accessible online. Three of the paper reports representing each of the steps in the status of an order—detailing the items requested but not yet ordered, the items currently on order, and the items received by the Acquisitions unit—were condensed into a single order status tab within the department's spreadsheet with a column for each report (see figure 10.1, p. 130). Each person in the workflow was assigned a specific column to keep current; for instance, one staff member was responsible for maintaining the requests presently on order. The careful construction of spreadsheet formulas allowed for the development of an account summary spreadsheet, displaying fiscal information about each account's activity and balance without adding to the weight of anyone's workload. Because the spreadsheet can be opened and edited by all of its users simultaneously, there is not any of the delay normally associated with shared files.

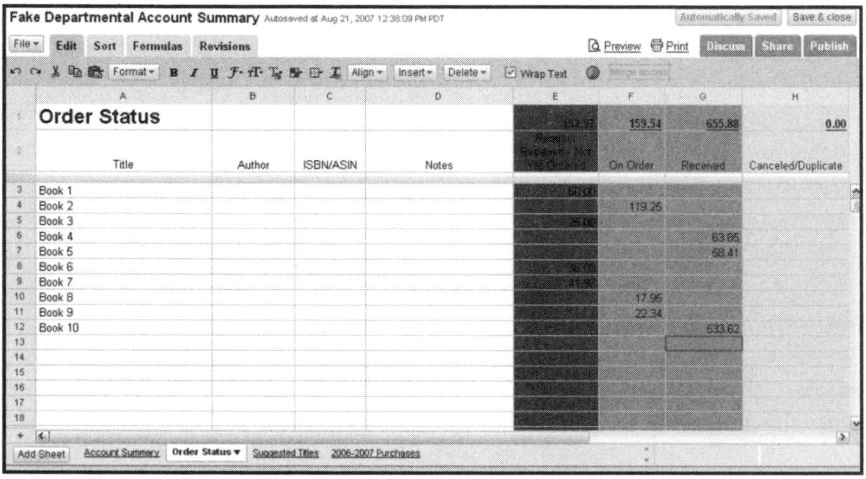

Figure 10.1. The "Order Status" Tab.

One of the issues Musser discusses in conjunction with harnessing collective intelligence is the lack of privacy. In an architecture of participation, especially where one person has responsibility for specific pieces of information, liability is an issue for both the user and the provider. Using the Google spreadsheets to deliver order status information to the department representatives also allows deans and department chairs to access that information. Similarly, department representatives have a greater insight into the steps of the ordering process. The removal of these barriers, can, however, ensure greater transparency in the overall operations of the library materials allocations. Departmental privacy is ensured by built-in functionality of Google spreadsheets. Only those sent an invitation can view the spreadsheet; by limiting the invitations for a particular department's spreadsheet to that department's dean, chair, representative, and liaison, only those people are able to view the activity and account summaries.

Harnessing collective intelligence, as the first of the *Web 2.0 Principles and Best Practices*, is also one of the most fundamental components of Web 2.0. Instead of compiling the fiscal and order status information from various people through one centralized person, the commonly edited spreadsheet allows people to update assigned sections, thus keeping the university community informed of fiscal and order status information on a constantly updated basis.

Data are the next "Intel Inside": "As the market shifts away from desktop applications for individuals and moves to a model of shared online services, it is becoming increasingly less about *function* alone, such as word-processing, and more about *data.* . . . For many online services, *the value is the data*" (Musser 2007, 21). A natural extension of "harnessing collective intelligence" is the utilization of unique data sources. Each person in the materials ordering workflow was already responsible for updating specific sets of data in the ILS. As mentioned previously, however, the ILS does not provide a method for displaying these data to the department representatives. Capitalizing on these data at the point of the individual responsible for them requires the addition of a step to each person's individual duties.

It was decided early in the development process to make the updates to the Google spreadsheets a daily occurrence, giving each dean, department chair, and department representative data that were newly generated based on the prior day's activity. Pulling the prior day's data from the ILS did not prove difficult; the difficulty lay in designing the spreadsheet to minimize the effort required of the staff whose responsibility it was to update the information. Originally, each of the three steps in the ordering process had its own separate tab in the spreadsheet, and each person was required to cut and paste the title from one tab to another as the title moved through the process. A semester-long usability test proved this method much too time consuming, resulting in a redesign and leading to the format outlined above (a single tab entitled "Order Status" with a separate column for each step in the process—updating each column being the responsibility of a specific person). As the workflow stands now, a report of the previous day's activity is distributed to each person, who then updates his or her defined portion of the spreadsheet.

Innovation in assembly: "Digital content lends itself to being taken apart and remixed" (Musser 2007, 27). Thus far, the *Web 2.0 Principles and Best Practices* have addressed the harnessing of collective intelligence to capitalize on unique data sources. How the data are presented is equally important. Web 2.0 allows for the construction of information systems to provide appropriate information tailored to users. As discussed previously, each person in the university community required different pieces of information. Whereas the department representatives needed to see order status, account summaries, cancellation notices, and reports of previous activities, the deans and department chairs were mostly concerned with fiscal information for their departments. Through the careful use of spreadsheet formulas, an "Account Summary" tab was provided as the opening tab of the spreadsheet. Each column in the "Order Status" tab had a simple SUM formula inserted at the top; as the column was updated as a result of Acquisitions activity, the total at the top changed. Because the location of this total remained static relative to the rest of the page, a transfer formula was used to copy the total information automatically to the "Account Summary" tab. With these automatic updates taking place as each Acquisitions staff member modified his or her column of responsibility, deans, department chairs, and department representatives could see account and deadline balances adjusting themselves instantly. The "Account Summary" tab includes an Acquisitions-only line to provide for balancing against the ILS. (See figure 10.2.)

Remixing data allows for the distribution of information to people with various information needs without requiring much hands-on activity after the initial design and setup.

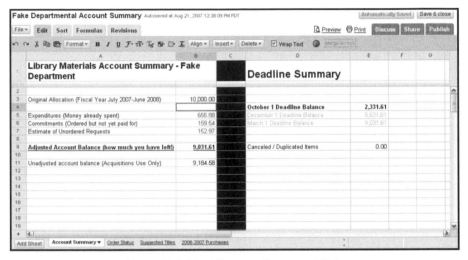

Figure 10.2. The "Account Summary" Tab.

Rich user experiences: "Deliver more compelling applications by leveraging the strengths of the desktop (i.e., rich interactivity, high user engagement, and fast performance) with the strengths of the network (i.e., platform independence, ubiquitous access, and collaboration)" (Musser 2007, 33). As the development of a "portal" for distributing Acquisitions' activity progressed, it became apparent that the portal could be used for much more.

As mentioned under "Institutional Profile," the department representatives —faculty in each academic department—are responsible for compiling and delivering requests for library purchases to expend each department's allocation. To facilitate this process, acquisitions and reference librarians would frequently provide collection development assistance to the departments. In the past, this was often limited to distributing trade catalogs or cards from *Choice Reviews*. Reference librarians also utilized *Resources for College Libraries* to generate lists of suggested titles appropriate for their assigned departments. To supplement these actions, the author turned to another Web 2.0 exemplar— LibraryThing.

LibraryThing is an online service that allows people to catalog their books. By searching for individual titles, people can build a catalog and tag what books they own, have borrowed, or are currently reading. LibraryThing can then make suggestions for further reading based on a number of different factors, such as

"Those who own the books in your library also own . . ." or "Similarly tagged books."

In the context of this case study, the Acquisitions unit created a LibraryThing account for each academic department, populated it with the titles of the books that department had requested in the previous fiscal year, and used the "suggestions" function to develop a list of similar titles. This list, along with price and ordering information, was provided to the departments via a tab in their Google spreadsheet labeled "Suggested Titles," to which the reference librarians were also allowed to add titles. The user name and password for the LibraryThing account was distributed to the department representatives for their own further use.

The combination of data that is of high interest to the user with a familiar interface allows the Google spreadsheet "portal" to enrich the users' experiences, giving them collection development assistance that is easily accessible from any Internet-connected devise.

Lightweight models and cost-effective scalability: "Changes in cost, reusability, process, and strategy mean much more can be done for much less" (Musser 2007, 51). One benefit of Web 2.0 technology is the general free access to the platform. Google Docs and Spreadsheets is completely free, while LibraryThing allows for the addition of up to 200 books on a free account. Although access costs may be free, labor costs must be considered. Much of the time involved in developing Murray State University Libraries' Web-based portal was spent either in development or data population. The design of the portal went through a number of iterations, each of which required serious planning and the careful application of formulas to make the best use of workflow patterns and staff. Each version underwent testing with those responsible for updating the spreadsheets and with a number of volunteer departments around campus. Once a design was agreed upon—one that delivered satisfactory information in a clear manner to the university community and remained logistically feasible for the acquisitions faculty and staff to maintain—a considerable amount of time was devoted to populating the spreadsheets with data appropriate to each department. Most of this data population was accomplished using a student worker over the summer, allowing the faculty and staff to continue with their normal responsibilities until the academic year started in late August. Once the initial data population was successfully completed, daily maintenance required approximately thirty minutes of each person responsible for a portion of the spreadsheets. Because the staff had been intimately involved in the developmental stages of the portal, they required little training once the portal went live. Training the university community took a good deal more time, but was accomplished through hosting training sessions, meeting one-on-one with the users, and the assistance of the library liaisons.

"Adoption of agile development processes, highly iterative product cycles, and tighter customer engagement reduce cost, time, and risk" (Musser 2007, 51).

As mentioned previously, the portal went through a number of versions before a design was finally accepted. Keeping the design of the portal "lightweight" was essential to making these changes, as each department's spreadsheet was completely isolated from those of all other departments. Once a decision to make a change was made, that change had to be carried out across all spreadsheets individually. Making the portal's design lightweight kept an extremely time- consuming process very efficient.

Murray State University Libraries use Google Docs and Spreadsheets in conjunction with LibraryThing to provide fiscal, order status, and collection development data to the university community, each level of which requires different combinations of the data. Web 2.0 technologies offer library technical service units the opportunity to accomplish a great deal through efficient and cost-effective means. By being commonly editable, they capitalize on the unique data for which each person is responsible, allowing the data to be remixed in ways that satisfy the users' information needs. Providing this remixed data can result in a richer experience for users and can be accomplished with a minimum of maintenance efforts.

Conclusion

This chapter set out to explore three questions:

- What is Web 2.0?

- How can libraries—specifically technical services—make use of Web 2.0 technology?

- What changes have to be made to technical services workflow to accommodate this new technology?

These three questions were explored through a case study examining the development and implementation of Web 2.0 technology in one academic library's Technical Services unit. The case study was undertaken using the *Web 2.0 Principles and Best Practices* developed by O'Reilly's John Musser as an analytic framework. The individual and interrelated components of the *Web 2.0 Principles and Best Practices* serve to answer the question "What is Web 2.0?" Web 2.0 is more than simply the natural evolution of the Internet; it is the harnessing of collective intelligence to capitalize on the unique data possessed by individuals in order to provide information that can be enriched by its very remixability.

How can libraries—specifically technical services—make use of Web 2.0 technology? As this case study pointed out, Web 2.0 can be utilized to fulfill a number of technical service demands. The Acquisitions unit of Murray State University Libraries utilizes Google Docs and Spreadsheets to distribute fiscal and order status information to a variety of people throughout the university community. It also utilizes LibraryThing to participate in collection development activities. How library technical services can utilize Web 2.0 is defined by their specific needs and is limited only by the creativity of those involved with workflow design.

What changes have to be made to technical services workflow to accommodate this new technology? By definition, Web 2.0 capitalizes on the energy, efforts, and knowledge of many people simultaneously. Murray State University was able—through much trial and error—to develop a workflow that both distributed the necessary information and remained logistically sustainable by the acquisitions faculty and staff. Carefully assigning various tasks to specific people ensured that the full weight of maintaining the "portal" did not fall too heavily on any one given person or group of people. This also kept the time required to perform those responsibilities to a minimum.

Various other units in the Murray State University Libraries system have adopted versions of Web 2.0 technology and adapted them to suit their individual needs. Policies and procedures are being compiled in a wiki, allowing everyone involved the opportunity to contribute. The minutes of meetings are being kept via shared documents on Google Docs and Spreadsheets, preventing the normal confusion resulting from editing and e-mailing files back and forth as the minutes are finalized. The author has plans to expand on the capabilities of the Acquisitions "portal," such as incorporating links to the catalog for the individual titles requested by the departments. As future needs arise, the application of Web 2.0 technology is likely to be a portion of any solution. Successfully implementing Web 2.0 as a solution to technical service issues requires only thorough planning and some creativity.

References

About LibraryThing. 2007. Available at www.librarything.com/about (accessed August 15, 2007).

Bolan, K., M. Canada, and R. Cullin. 2007. Web, library, and teen services 2.0. *Young Adult Library Services* 5 (2) (Winter): 40–43.

Coombs, K. A. 2007. Building a library Web site on the pillars of Web 2.0. *Computers in Libraries* 27 (1) (January): 17–19.

Dubon, B. 2006. Web 2.0. *AIIM E-Doc Magazine* 20 (6) (November/December): 64.

Dye, J. 2007. Collaboration 2.0: Make the web your workspace. *EContent* 30 (1) (January/February): 32–36.

Hauser, J. 2007. Media specialists can learn Web 2.0 tools to make schools more cool. *Computers in Libraries* 27 (2) (February): 6–8, 47–48.

Huffman, K. 2006. Web 2.0: beyond the concept: Practical ways to implement RSS, Podcasts, and Wikis. *Education Libraries* 29 (1) (Summer): 12–19.

Kemp, R. 2007. Catalog/cataloging changes and Web 2.0 functionality: New directions for serials. *The Serials Librarian* 53 (4) (January): 91–112.

Maness, J. M. 2006. Library 2.0: The next generation of web-based library services. *Logos* 17 (3), 139–45.

Musser, J. 2007. *Web 2.0: Principles and best practices*. Sebastopol, CA: O'Reilly Radar.

Notess, G. R. 2006a. The terrible twos: Web 2.0, Library 2.0 and more. *Online 30* (3) (May/June): 40–42.

Notess, G. R. 2006b. Diverging web markup choices. *Online 30* (6) (November/December): 43–45.

Stephens, M. 2006. Dispatches from the field: The promise of Web 2.0. *American Libraries* 37 (9) (October): 32.

Szomszor, M., C. Cattuto, H. Alani, et al. 2007. Folksonomies, the semantic web, and movie recommendation. In *Proceedings of 4th European Semantic Web Conference, bridging the gap between semantic Web and Web 2.0.* Innsbruck, Austria. Available at eprints.ecs.soton.ac.uk/14007/ (accessed September 4, 2008).

Index

137

About the Editor and Contributors

Editor

Bradford Lee Eden is Associate University Librarian for Technical Services and Scholarly Communication at the University of California, Santa Barbara. Previous positions include Head, Web and Digitization Services, for the University of Nevada, Las Vegas Libraries; Head, Bibliographic and Metadata Services for the UNLV Libraries; as well as Coordinator of Technical Services for the North Harris Montgomery Community College District. He is editor of *OCLC Systems & Services: Digital Library Perspectives International* and *The Bottom Line: Managing Library Finances*, and is associate editor of *Library Hi Tech* and *The Journal of Film Music*. He has a master's and Ph.D. degrees in musicology, as well as an M.S. in library science. He publishes in the areas of metadata, librarianship, medieval music and liturgy, and J. R. R. Tolkien. He edited *Innovative Redesign and Reorganization of Library Technical Services: Paths for the Future and Case Studies* (Libraries Unlimited, 2004) and is the author of *Metadata and Its Applications* (ALA TechSource, 2002), *3D Visualization Techniques* (ALA TechSource, 2005), *Innovative Digital Projects in the Humanities* (ALA TechSource, 2005), *Metadata and Its Applications: New Directions and Updates* (ALA TechSource, 2005), *FRBR: Functional Requirements for Bibliographic Records* (ALA TechSource, 2006), and *Information Organization Future for Libraries* (ALA TechSource, 2007).

Contributors

Michael Aulich is Director, Access and Delivery, Information Services, Australian Taxation Office, a position he has held for three years. Previously he was Senior Coordinator, Systems Processes and Archives at Brisbane City Council Library Services, for six years.

Elizabeth Brice earned her M.L.S. from Indiana University, Bloomington, after receiving her B.A. in history from Beloit College, Wisconsin. She began her career at Miami University in Oxford, Ohio, cataloging rare books as Special Collections Librarian. She has served as Head of Technical Services for the past ten years and as Interim Assistant Dean for the past three.

Michael Garrett is Technology Coordinator at the HAM–TMC Library. In that capacity, he is responsible for the development of technology solutions throughout the entire Library. He graduated from the University of North Texas School of Library and Information Science and is a certified Adobe ColdFusion MX Developer.

Dean James is Print Resources and Metadata Coordinator at the HAM–TMC Library. He holds a Ph.D. in medieval history from Rice University and an M.S.L.S. from the University of North Texas School of Library and Information Science. From 1986 through 1996 he was a part of the Cataloging Department, eventually becoming Director of Cataloging and Serials. After a nine-year absence, he returned to the Library in January 2006.

Kate Lyons is Reference and Information Technology Librarian at Hostos Community College of the City University of New York (CUNY). She holds an M.S. in management from the Wagner School of Public Service at New York University, an M.S. in library and information science from the University of Illinois at Urbana-Champaign, and a B.A. in English from Grinnell College.

Christine Mackenzie is the CEO of Yarra Plenty Regional Library Service, Melbourne, Australia, a position she has held for three years. Prior to this she was Manager of Library Services at Brisbane City Council for six years. Christine is a past president of the Australian Library and Information Association and has held executive positions on various ALIA sections and branches. She has been chair of a number of committees, including the Public Libraries Advisory Committee of the Library Board of Queensland and Viclink. She was a member of the Bertelsmann Foundation's International Network of Public Libraries and is currently a committee member of the International Federation of Library Association's Metropolitan Libraries Section.

Adam Murray is a recent graduate of University of North Carolina at Greensboro's M.L.I.S. program. Having completed his degree in the summer of 2006, he became Murray State University Libraries' first Head of Acquisitions in eight years. One year later, he was appointed Interim Dean of University Libraries, the youngest ever to hold that position at Murray State.

Karen A. Nuckolls is Head of Technical Services at the University of Kentucky Evans Law Library. Previously she held similar positions in other academic libraries, a public library system in New York, and a law firm in Philadelphia. She has over thirty years' experience in technical services and management and has presented talks on these topics at several conferences.

Laurie Phillips is Associate Dean for Technical Services at the J. Edgar & Louise S. Monroe Library at Loyola University New Orleans, where she has served in various technical services positions since being hired as Music and Media Cataloger in 1990.

Laurel Sanders was Serials Librarian at the HAM–TMC Library between 1999 and 2007 and is now the Electronic Resources Coordinator. She is a 1994 graduate of the Louisiana State University School of Library and Information Science.

Roxanne Sellberg has been a manager of library technical services operations for over twenty years. After earning her M.L.S. at UCLA in 1979, she spent her early career specializing in cataloging and database management; her publications and service record reflect this interest. She held positions of increasing administrative responsibility at the University of Nebraska–Lincoln, Indiana University, and the University of Washington. While at Indiana University she earned a specialist degree in academic library administration. She came to Northwestern University in 1995 to be head of technical services operations in the University Library. As part of a recent library reorganization, she has become Assistant University Librarian for Technical Services and Resource Management there.

Ross Shanley-Roberts earned both his B.A. in English and Spanish language and literature and his master's of medieval studies from Western Michigan University, and his master's of library science from Indiana University, Bloomington. He was the Cataloger for the NEH Microfilming Project in the Medieval Institute at the University of Notre Dame and the Jesuitana Cataloger at the John J. Burns Library at Boston College, and has served in numerous positions at Miami University, Oxford, Ohio, including Authority Control Librarian, Head of the Digital Processing Unit, and Assistant Head of Technical Services.

Daniel Sifton is a graduate of the School of Information Management at Dalhousie University in Halifax, Nova Scotia. Since 2004 he has been the Coordinator of Support Services for the Cariboo Regional District Library in Williams Lake, British Columbia.

Vicki Toy Smith is principal cataloger at the University of Nevada, Reno. She has previously worked at Proquest Learning and Information (UMI), the University of Michigan, and the University of California, Berkeley. Vicki has an A.M.L.S. from the University of Michigan, an M.A. from Eastern Michigan, and an A.B. from the University of California, Berkeley. She publishes articles on the topics of metadata and library science and is president of OLAC.

Elisabeth Tappeiner is the Head of Technical Services and Collection Development at Hostos Community College of the City University of New York (CUNY). She holds an M.A. in comparative literature, an M.A. in library and information studies from the University of Wisconsin–Madison, and a B.A. in French and history from the University of Minnesota–Twin Cities.